Super Pres

Hull

John Banks

Cover: For many years Hull bought bus bodywork from Weymann's Motor Bodies, of Addlestone, Surrey, and in the postwar period the typical blue and white double-decker on the city's streets was a Weymann-bodied AEC Regent. Most had exposed radiators, including a batch of 20 eight-feet-wide versions delivered in 1950. They lasted in service up to 1968/9 and one of the 1969 withdrawals, and the highest-numbered of the batch, is seen in the last weeks of its working life. Number **335** (**KRH 345**) was in Ings Road at the Tweendykes Road terminus of route 33 on 25th April 1969. *(Philip Battersby)*

Rear cover: Hull had only 16 "Coronation" trolleybuses: the 1953 prototype and a batch of 15 production machines bought in 1954/5. They were destined for a very short working life in Hull up to the abandonment of the trolleybus system and were scrapped when barely a decade old. They were very familiar to users of the 61/62/63 group of routes operated by Cottingham Road garage, inside which No. **109** (**RKH 109**) is seen in about 1955. It is in the process of having an advertisement for a football pool applied by a left-handed signwriter. *(L R Storry)*

Inside front cover: A publicity poster celebrating 90 years of the Hull municipal passenger transport undertaking that appeared on street hoardings in 1989. *(John Banks)*

Inside rear cover: In the later postwar period the Leyland Atlantean took over from the AEC Regent as the typical Hull bus. This was a late example, dating from 1975. Number **360** (**GAT 199N**) was at the outer terminus of route 57 in 1979. *(John Banks)*

Title page: A nostalgic view of the junction of Jameson Street with Prospect Street (to the left) and King Edward Street in 1954. Weymann-bodied AEC Regents, including one of the 1953 concealed radiator examples, No. **338** (**OKH 338**), predominate, with a trolleybus on the 64 Holderness Road route just visible in the bottom corner and an East Yorkshire Roe-bodied Leyland Titan PD1 in the distance. *(Hull Daily Mail)*

Opposite page: Monument Bridge looking into Queen Victoria Square in the early 1930s. The Guy FCX six-wheeled bus, No. **59** (**RH 1282**), was new in June 1930 and withdrawn in 1937. It had a 62-seat body by Brush Coachworks, of Loughborough. The original position of the Wilberforce monument is clearly shown, as are the relative positions of, from left to right, the City Hall, the Queen Victoria statue, the buildings at the corner of King Edward Street/Waterworks Street and the Dock Office, whose clock shows that the picture was taken at ten minutes past midday. The picture dates from after June 1932 and before 1935. *(Hull Daily Mail)*

Below: Variety at the rear of Holderness Road depot in the 1950s. Three wartime Guy Arabs, Nos **234**, **206**, and **215** (**GRH 379**, **GKH 519** and **GRH 130**), all either rebodied or substantially rebuilt, share the parking area with AEC Regent No. **282** (**KAT 282**) of 1949. *(L R Storry)*

INTRODUCTION

Youthful memories

It is difficult to look dispassionately at one's home town, especially when one moved away from it as soon as one reasonably could. Memories of it are sometimes good, sometimes bad, often indifferent. The good ones include the bus fleets: East Yorkshire, the various independents and - the Corporation. Whatever it is that causes a youngster to turn an interest in public transport fleets into a lifelong hobby, it is certainly his local fleets, to which he is perforce attached in a proprietorial way, that form the bedrock.

The writer was born in the darkest days of the Second World War when Kingston upon Hull was being liberally pounded by German bombers: thus much was changing or disappearing even as the child began to sit up and take notice as the war ended and postwar austerity set in.

Many were the dreadful stories of the war and of the City told later over the fireside by parents to a shivering stripling: how, for example, a police officer had been seen walking along Ferensway just before a bomb hit and nothing was ever found of him save the numerals from his uniform tunic. Their stories ranged wider than simply the war, though, and the young listener - already aware of the city's bus and trolleybus fleet and with a solitary, though sharp and clear, memory of the trams - was outraged to be told that when Queen's Gardens in the city centre was made from the no longer needed Queen's Dock, the hole was filled in with, among other things, a number of old buses (as well as - and even now the mind still boggles - tipper-lorries full of old telephones). It was fascinating to learn that youngsters, before the war, would take the

Early days of the electric trams. A scene at Princes Avenue junction with Spring Bank in about 1905. The latter thoroughfare was to the right, and led to the city centre - or "town" as we always knew it. The stationary traffic indicates that the level crossing gates - just out of view, but their shadow can be seen on the road - were closed to allow the passage of a train. The buildings on the right are those of Botanic Gardens railway station whence we would depart for days at the seaside in the pre-Beeching era. Tram No. 116 was a 1903 Milnes 56-seater. Among the other traffic there is a splendid cameo of a cheeky cyclist supporting himself against the side of the tram to avoid having to put his feet down. The motor car has yet to make its presence felt. (John Banks Collection)

Hedon Road tram to its terminus and then *walk* the rest of the way to the seaside, which at its closest must have been a dozen miles away

The trams for the writer, as was said, account for just one rather vivid memory. Father decided, one day in 1945, to go for a haircut, and for reasons now unknown decided to take his three-year-old son with him. In those days it was safe for a child to be left unattended outside the barber's shop in Osbourne Street, and I recall watching a stationary tram for some minutes. It must have been at the town end of the Hessle Road "D" route, for all the others had gone by then: indeed, the "D" ceased on 30th June 1945; I was three and a bit, then, and that memory is a cherished one.

We moved around a lot. I lived in six different houses until I left for London at the age of 18; in that time I attended only three schools, and in travelling to and from them made much use of the trolleybuses. As a young boy I was forbidden to ride on the "petrol buses" for two reasons: the fares were more expensive (up to 1951 a child could ride all or part of any trolleybus route for a flat fare of ½d - 1d thence to 1953; this was a concession that was not available on the motorbuses); and because in the late afternoon many of the motorbus routes became Limited Stop. They would not set down passengers until beyond the outer termini of the trolleybus routes - but they

would pick up. Because the motorbuses were forbidden, naturally we used them. But it was a gamble at Limited Stop time: you stood on the platform and hoped that somebody at your stop

The writer's solitary memory of a route "D" tramcar must have been of an occasion before 30th June 1945, when the Hessle Road tram route (the last) was withdrawn. Why was Hessle Road known as "D" on the trams? Well, the outer terminus was at a place on the outskirts known as Dairycoates, as indicated on much-rebuilt 1912 car No. **144** *(above). Number* **113** *(right) was in the charge of Driver Alf Fellows and a youthful companion on 1st December 1944. This car dated in this form from 1925, built (or reconstructed - the evidence is conflicting) as a replacement car by Hull Corporation, and was fitted with new trucks in the early thirties. (John Banks Collection; Hull Daily Mail)*

The Ravages of War

In these before and after views of Queen Victoria Square, looking along King Edward Street, with Savile Street on the right and Waterworks Street on the left, the terminal point for Beverley Road and Spring Bank trams can be seen (above) in a bustling prewar scene. In the picture below the monarch had survived on her pedestal but all that she surveyed had changed beyond recognition. In addition to the enemy bombs intended for the city, it also received the attentions of bombers returning from other cities unloading what weapons of destruction they retained as they passed over Hull, the last target before the open sea on the way back to Germany. (John Banks Collection)

The same scene, from a little way further back, well into the postwar years. The City Hall and the Dock Offices, at left and right, had survived in more or less original condition, but the premises in King Edward Street and Waterworks Street (renamed in 1952 as a continuation of Paragon Street) were new from the foundations up. The trams in King Edward Street are long gone, replaced by trolleybuses, some of which are visible at the service 61 (Chanterlands Avenue), 62 (Newland Avenue) and 63 (Beverley Road) terminal stands. The 69 (Anlaby Road) and 70 (Hessle Road) routes had their stands out of view alongside the City Hall. The 64 (Holderness Road) for its first six months terminated in Savile Street and also turned in the Square but from August 1940 to 1959 passed through on inward journeys only to reach its terminus in Jameson Street, some distance beyond the City Hall and close to the railway station. Trolleybuses on all those routes thus negotiating Queen Victoria Square to pick up their outward timings meant a constant stream of them throughout the day. Had the resources been available, the entire trolleybus fleet could have been photographed in one part or another of this picturesque location. "Of all sad words of tongue or pen, the saddest are these: 'it might have been' ". (John Banks Collection)

would hail the bus. The entirely foreseeable result was that you were often carried on one, two or several stops beyond yours. The trolleybus terminated perhaps a quarter-mile from home - the gamble lay in hoping that the motorbus would take you on not more than that distance before having to stop to pick up. It didn't always work...

Using the buses was one thing, exploring their garages and other hideaways was quite

another. The local depots at Cottingham Road and Holderness Road were quite easy to get into; the latter had open parking at the back, in which withdrawn stock was often to be seen. Memory suggests that it was not so easy to wangle one's way into Wheeler Street trolleybus depot, and it certainly was not easy to find a way into Central in Lombard Street. And as for Liverpool Street works... Still, we did what we could in pursuance of our interest,

HULL CORPORATION

again increases
its Fleet of LEYLANDS by

TEN 'TITANS'

Leyland

LEYLAND, LANCS.

<< Opposite page: In a trade press advertisement placed by Leyland Motors in August 1932, one of the Corporation's TD2 Titans with Leyland highbridge 48-seat bodywork, is seen in Queen Victoria Square. Trams in King Edward Street can again be seen, as can the buildings at the corner of that thoroughfare and Waterworks Street. The wording of the advertisement is somewhat disingenuous, as the vehicle, fleet number **107** (**TF 7819**), was, with the rest of the claimed batch of ten, merely on loan from Leyland Motors until they were purchased in 1934, at which time this one was renumbered 121. (John Banks Collection)*

an interest which, incidentally, met with a total lack of comprehension by parents.

I left the city in 1961 and so was spared the one-man operation revolution and could only mourn from afar as the trolleybuses were gradually run down, with that well-remembered Beverley High Road route - the 63 - being the last to go. Circumstances took me back to Hull for a decade or so in the seventies and eighties, but I was again absent from the traumas of deregulation and sale of the undertaking.

All the above is, of course, subjective: the memories are of my childhood and formative years, so how could it not be? Enough of that, though: let us now try for an objective overview of the city and of its public transport by road.

The name

In this whole *Prestige* and *Super Prestige* series of transport history picture albums, it is a safe bet that no other will have a title shorter than this one. Yet choosing that title was not as easy as might first appear. The proper title "Kingston upon Hull" would distract readers to Surrey or Jamaica just at the moment when we wanted them to think of Hull. The more sonorous "Hull Corporation" would specify clearly the undertaking featured in these pages, but its name did not always include the word Corporation. The initials KHCT were very widely used for many decades, yet are a somewhat localised shorthand which is not appropriate as a title in these circumstances. So Hull it is, whether that strikes you unfavourably because of media prejudice, or whether you recognize it for what it is, an old, proud and large Yorkshire city which was Britain's third port (after London and Liverpool) for well over 150 years until radical changes in trade altered the balance in quite recent times.

The river

Despite the city's proper title, the River Hull is almost unknown outside the immediate area, yet it is the reason for the city's existence, and the need to cross it has set a pattern on the local transport system. It rises in the wolds at Driffield, hardly 100 feet above sea level and only some twenty miles north of the city. Today you can stand at the Pier in Nelson Street near what was for so long a tram, bus and ferry terminus, watch the waters of the Hull flowing into the mighty but treacherous Humber, and reflect that the whole city exists because of this. The River Hull provided a haven at the very point where the waters of the Humber ran deepest, an important factor where shifting sandbanks are an ever present threat to shipping. There was a settlement recorded here in the Domesday Book in 1086 and a flourishing port by 1193. King Edward I bought the lands of the two districts then known as Wyke and Myton in 1293, thereby owning the port as a Royal estate, the King's Town upon Hull. Eventually, in 1440, it became an independent borough - which would one day become a transport operator.

Links with the past

There is a clear link between 1440 and the municipal transport system. The church of St Mary, Lowgate, was enlarged in the 15th century. Its stained glass included the coat of arms of the new borough of Kingston upon Hull, which very simply consisted of three crowns to designate the royal antecedent. That stained glass is still there. This is particularly worthy of comment in a city which was very heavily bombed during the second world war, as we shall mention later. The three crowns emblem was carried by all the municipal trams and buses for over 94 years, latterly in a very clear and prominent design. Liveries on the

The Endike Lane Terminus

*The writer attended infant and junior schools in Hull's Endike Lane in the forties and fifties. That thoroughfare was to the left of the vehicles in these pictures and his home was about a quarter-mile further along Beverley High Road - a fine, dual carriageway with reserved central tram tracks. In the upper picture cars Nos **124** and **125** are seen in 1937 not long before the "B" route finished on 3rd September 1938. Built in the Corporation's workshops in 1909/10, these 56-seat cars were rebuilt as fully enclosed 62-seaters in the 1920s The prototype Sunbeam MF2B Roe-bodied, dual-doorway, 54-seat trolleybus, No. **101 (NRH 101)**, stands at the replacing trolleybus route terminus at the same location in 1963 (below) where trolleybuses turned through a gap in the dual-carriageway central reservation - a legacy of the trams and their reserved tracks. The vehicle had been exhibited at the 1952 Commercial Motor Show and entered service in 1953. It was withdrawn in 1964 upon abandonment of the trolleybus system and sold for scrap. (Hull Daily Mail; John Banks Collection)*

vehicles changed from time to time, and the coat of arms was thus their enduring distinguishing feature.

The city in modern times

The visitor's first task is to reach the city, for he is unlikely to come to Hull on the way to anywhere else except for the Rotterdam and Zeebrugge ferries. The main railway line, and to a lesser extent the M62/A63 road, run along the shores of the Humber as it comes in from the west. Arrival at the city's Paragon terminal station is accompanied by a strong impression of having reached the end of the line, especially as the railways from the coast, which is even further east, have always come round the northern suburbs to enter the station from the west. If "the end of the line" is a physical fact, it is even more strongly psychological, and Hull has a distinctive character arising from many centuries of relative isolation, if not from the mainstream of national life, at least from the flow of its traffic. The local transport system has therefore always been self contained. In the tramway years, the neighbouring systems were Doncaster, York, and Scarborough, all some 40-50 miles distant and all effectively nearer than Grimsby, only 11 miles away for the proverbial crow but on the Lincolnshire side of the Humber. A hovercraft service was introduced between Hull and Grimsby in 1969 but was remarkably short-lived. The age-old isolation had in fact been ended by the railways 150 years ago for those who could afford to travel, and it has long been possible to reach Leeds, York, Doncaster or Scarborough in little over an hour from Hull.

The usual pattern of growth and development gradually created a city of some 300,000 people. The names of many cities have become synonymous with a single industry, such as coal, steel, cotton or wool, usually because of available natural resources. In this way, Hull will forever be associated with fish, but the city has always had a great diversity of other industry arising from the variety of imports over the centuries.

Unlike Plymouth, Portsmouth and Southampton with their convoluted coastlines and waterfronts, Hull's geography is simplicity itself. The D-shaped city has a straight south-facing shoreline and is bisected by the River Hull. The land is flat and subject to flooding, features which resulted first in the construction of extensive land drains ('drains' in Hull are what would be called dykes anywhere else), then in a multiplicity of railway level crossings in the 19th century, and much more recently in the striking structure of the tidal barrier at the mouth of the River Hull.

The city's radiating roads

Now that you have been introduced, it is time to look around. Your train or your express coach will set you down in the very centre of the city, on the west side of the river. The modern Interchange notion came to Hull in 1935 with the opening of the grandly named Coach Station (actually the bus station) in an ideal position immediately next to the railway station. Unlike many other places where bus stations have been closed and sold and buses relegated to loading in the streets, Hull has determinedly kept this important facility. As you start to get your bearings, you will find that the main roads radiate from the city centre like the spokes of half a wheel. These roads dominate the life of the city and the provision of its transport services. Indeed, for many years trolleybuses and motorbuses displayed no final destination but simply, for example, "via Beverley Road", with the actual terminus being denoted by the number. The visitor would begin by wondering "Why don't they show the name of the district or locality to which they are going?", but would soon find out that in many cases the districts simply didn't have names, other than existing settlements such as Sculcoates, Stoneferry and Sutton which had been absorbed as the city expanded. Nor do they yet, or to be more precise, the name of the main road is the district name - "Holderness Road" or "Newland Avenue" is the area in which you live rather than the street where your house is. The city falls naturally into three parts known prosaically as West Hull, North Hull and East Hull, too amorphous to serve as terminus names, and subdivided by the above-mentioned main roads. District names slowly came into daily use only as modern housing estates were built. With the growth of frequent bus services to estates such as Gipsyville and

Spring Bank West

A later home was on the tree- and cemetery-lined road that connected Botanic Gardens, with its level crossing and suburban railway station, with outlying areas to the north-west of the city. Spring Bank West had had its tram route, the "SW", from 1913 to 1934; and its trolleybus services 61 and 65 to Chanterlands Avenue North/Cottingham Road and Goddard Avenue respectively. From the motorbus era, in pictures taken from the writer's front doorstep, are two generations of motorbus. Number 193 (GKH 374) (above) was a 1942 AEC Regent of the type known as "unfrozen". Upon the outbreak of war all bus production was frozen by Whitehall decree; later, buses already in build at the time of the decree, or those that could be completed from stocks of parts already in existence, were authorised, or "unfrozen", and thus they were known ever afterwards. This one originally had a Brush 56-seat body, replaced in 1951 with the similar, but Massey, of Wigan, built body from 1939 AEC Regent No. 172. In this summer 1961 view it had a little less than two years to go before its withdrawal. Below, in the same place about 15 years later, was 1969 Leyland Atlantean No. 251 (PRH 251G). The out-and-back 15 route to Greenwood Avenue had by then become the Orchard Park Estate circular 15C. (Both: John Banks)

Longhill, Hull buses gradually took on a more conventional appearance by showing these names, but the old style died hard when it came to the likes of "Ings Road Estate".

The horse trams

It was only to be expected that the first transport services should have followed these main roads, 'the spokes of the wheel'. The first horse-tram service commenced in 1875, and after an uncertain beginning a network of routes was operated by the Hull Street Tramways Company from 1877. There was only one route to the east, along Holderness Road, reached by crossing the North Bridge over the busy River Hull - there had been a bridge here since 1541. The short 1877 tramway to the Pier negotiated another such structure at Monument Bridge, necessary because the development of the three Town Docks by 1829 meant that the historic Old Town was encircled by water. Generations of late schoolchildren and broken appointments were habitually to be explained with the words "the bridge was up". As for the monument, this imposing pillar (moved to Queen's Gardens in 1935) commemorates William Wilberforce, born 1759, the internationally famous slave trade reformer who is Hull's greatest son.

A second route eastwards had been proposed, along Hedon Road, which nowadays carries very heavy traffic to King George Dock. In the 1870s this area was undeveloped and the horse-tramway was not built, but the situation changed radically with the opening of the Hull & Barnsley Railway's Alexandra Dock in 1885. The opportunity was promptly taken up by a new local enterprise, the Drypool and Marfleet Steam Tramway Company, although it was 1889 before their line along Hedon Road commenced operations. This tramway did not cross the River Hull, but terminated on the east side of North Bridge and also had a short spur to the newly constructed Drypool Bridge of 1888.

The horse tramway system ran successfully for over a decade but was seriously hampered by its single-track layout and by intense competition from horse wagonettes. The Hull Street Tramways Company failed in 1889 and the undertaking ran for some years under the auspices of the receiver. In this difficult period the cars were kept quite well, but the track deteriorated seriously.

The Corporation purchased the horse tramway in 1896 and leased it to local cab proprietor W Nettleton. By this time electric tramways with overhead current collection were operating successfully in, for example, Leeds, South Staffordshire, Bristol, the Hartlepools and Dublin, and after some debate the Corporation set its sights firmly on the new form of traction. Accordingly, the first rail of a new system was laid in 1898 and electric cars took over the reconstructed Anlaby Road and Hessle Road routes in 1899. For a short while the city could boast of having horse, steam and electric trams simultaneously, but the last horse cars ran later that year.

Electric trams

For 1900, the Holderness Road, Spring Bank and Beverley Road routes were relaid, electrified and extended. This left the steam-operated Hedon Road line, purchased by the Corporation in January 1900 and run for a further twelve months, to be converted to electric traction, but in the event it was December 1903 before the line reopened, with the service extended inwards via the existing (Holderness Road) tracks over North Bridge and into the city centre. Another long-delayed line also reopened in 1903, to the Pier via the Old Town but rerouted via the newly built Alfred Gelder Street. These were busy and expensive years for the Corporation. In one sense, the tramway network was much as before, with the system operating along the main roads in the same 'spokes of a wheel' formation. In another sense, immense progress had been made, with the routes variously extended along these same roads, double tracked throughout, electrically operated, and providing an intensive service with the aid of a much larger fleet than hitherto. At long last, the overwhelming competition suffered from horse buses and wagonettes was vanquished.

The town was raised to city status in 1897, so it was hardly surprising that the new Corporation cars, all double-deckers, were lettered "City of Hull Tramways". The system was distinguished by its centre-groove rails,

HULL CORPORATION TRAM SERVICES

Date commenced	Route letter/s	Route	Last day of service
5th July 1899	A	Anlaby Road (Wheeler Street)	5th September 1942
5th July 1899	D	Hessle Road (Dairycoates)	30th June 1945
10th April 1900	H	Holderness Road (Lee Street)	17th February 1940
2nd June 1900	S	Spring Bank (Botanic Gardens)	24th July 1937
8th October 1900	S	Botanic Gardens to Queens Road	24th July 1937
8th December 1900	B	Beverley Road (Cottingham Road)	3rd September 1938
19th January 1903	S	Queens Road to Newland Avenue top	24th July 1937
27th March 1903	H	Holderness Road (Lee Street to Aberdeen Street)	17th February 1940
20th October 1903	P	Pier	5th September 1931
17th December 1903	M	Hedon Road (Drain Bridge)	1st January 1938
29th July 1907	TH	Town Hall to Holderness Road	27th June 1932
29th April 1912	MA	Hedon Road (Drain Bridge to Marfleet Avenue)	1st January 1938
9th October 1913	SW	Spring Bank West (Botanic Gardens to level crossing, Walton Street)	28th July 1934
16th February 1914	DP	Hessle Road (Dairycoates to Pickering Park Gates)	28th July 1934
14th July 1919	BC	Cottingham Road (Beverley Road to Newland Park east entrance)	28th July 1934
7th September 1925	H	Holderness Road (Aberdeen Street to Ings Road)	17th February 1940
5th October 1925	DP	Hessle High Road (Pickering Park Gates to Pickering Road)	28th July 1934
5th October 1925	AP	Anlaby High Road (Wheeler Street to Pickering Road)	28th July 1934
5th October 1925	SW	Chanterlands Avenue South	28th July 1934
5th October 1925	BC	Cottingham Road (Newland Park east to Goodfellowship Inn)	28th July 1934
12th July 1926	B	Beverley High Road (Cottingham Road to Endike Lane)	3rd September 1938
3rd January 1927	SWC	Chanterlands Avenue North	28th July 1934

Route letter MA was subsequently discontinued, with all Hedon Road cars displaying M.

Route letters QS (short working of S to Queens Road) and BN (short working of B, turning in Cottingham Road (Newland)) were also used.

A short length of reserved track was built beyond Wheeler Street as a terminal stub in Boothferry Road for service A cars when the route was extended as AP along Anlaby High Road. This remained in use until the end of the A service.

intended to make possible a smoother ride by having two running surfaces for each wheel. In the electric era, this feature was otherwise found only at Doncaster. There were 100 four-wheel electric trams in Hull by the end of 1901, including the 25 trailers of 1899 motorised in 1900. Car 101 was the only bogie car. Route letters were introduced in 1902 - A for Anlaby Road, B for Beverley Road, etc. - and lasted until the end of the system; their prominent display on the cars was a distinctive feature not commonly found elsewhere. The first covered-top cars came in 1903, and the whole fleet was so fitted by 1909. The fleet reached a maximum of 180 in 1915 but the following year dropped to 179 when car 101 was sold to Erith. Continued development saw extension of most of the routes, in many cases along fine reserved tracks, accompanied by the modernisation of the cars. By 1935 almost the whole fleet was enclosed, many had upholstered seating, and a large number had received more modern trucks and equipment, notably including much purchased from Rochdale and from the unfortunate Dearne District system. One remarkable development under manager Mr E S Rayner was the experimental tram of 1923 which took the vacant number 101; the truck incorporated cardan drive shafts and differentials, and the body was totally enclosed, with an ingenious staircase and platform arrangement resembling that which was later familiar in Edinburgh. The car was the centre of attention at the Tramway Managers' Conference, held in Hull that year, and a large-scale model of it was shown at the British Empire Exhibition at Wembley in 1924.

The first motorbuses

Meanwhile a newcomer had made its appearance - the Corporation motor bus. Construction of a tramway to Stoneferry had actually begun, and some rails laid, but the scheme was abandoned and a bus service introduced in 1909. The vehicles were Saurer open-top double-deckers which had a chequered career, and the service ceased in 1912. A fresh start was made with three AEC K-types in 1921, augmented by a number of Bristol vehicles in 1923. Considerable motorbus development in the 1920s provided services to districts in between the tram routes and beyond them, the needs increasing as large scale council house construction commenced under the provisions of the 1919 Housing Act. This coincided with rapid technical advance in bus design, and the fleet grew remarkably in this decade, from nothing to 55 in the ten years to the end of 1930, by which time the buses were approaching one-third of the trams' fleet strength. The development of low frames, pneumatic tyres and fully-enclosed double-deckers transformed bus design from primitive

to civilised in little more than five years. As happened elsewhere, the fleet intake was remarkably varied, with Guy for a while being the principal choice although AEC, Bristol and Leyland featured prominently.

In 1931 the new man at the top was Mr D P Morrison, who had been in charge at Dundee for five years and had previously been the engineer at Gateshead where his father had been general manager. Whilst he was leaving a city which would retain its predominantly tramway outlook for over twenty years more, his arrival in Hull caused (or coincided with) the development of the opposite viewpoint. The Hull Corporation Tramways title had been in use from about 1920, but now the 'Tramways' became 'Transport', and the short route to the Pier was replaced by motorbuses. In 1932 discussions commenced with East Yorkshire Motor Services with a view to coordinating the two undertakings, and the buses, hitherto maroon like the trams, became blue and white like the buses in Dundee. Nevertheless, the work of tramcar refurbishment continued for some three years more.

A change in the city centre occurred in 1931 when a wide new road was completed through what had been a maze of poor streets to link Anlaby Road and the railway station with Beverley Road. It was named Ferensway in memory of city benefactor T R Ferens (1847-1930). The existence of this road was conducive to the construction not only of the Coach Station but also of a new Central Garage and Head Office for the Corporation Transport in the adjacent Lombard Street. All these premises opened in 1935.

The motorbus fleet had doubled in five years, from 55 at the end of 1930 to 110 at the end of 1935. Many earlier vehicles were also replaced, so that the intake in these five years totalled 86, made up principally of 32 AEC, 28 Leyland and 22 Daimler. A surprisingly large number of hired vehicles was operated, some on brief loan as demonstrators, others on longer-term hire, with many of the latter ultimately being purchased. The balance comprised four Dennis double-deckers which were to be the last of that make for over fifty years. The most notable purchases were all from AEC, a double-deck Q, ten Regal single-deckers, and the first oil-engined (diesel) bus.

The area agreement

The agreement reached with East Yorkshire was implemented on 29th July 1934. It was a model operating agreement that stood the test of time and led the way for similar agreements in places such as Brighton, Plymouth and Newcastle: yet on the other hand it could be interpreted as spelling the end for the tramways. This was not the Bristol or Scarborough type of agreement where the company operated all the services on behalf of the Corporation; rather, it provided mutual protection for two distinct operators who ran alongside each other over a comprehensive urban network. The agreement created three operating areas known as A (inner), B (suburban) and C (outer). All revenue from area A went to the Corporation and from area C to East Yorkshire, with the revenue from area B shared between the parties. This division of receipts was balanced by a division of working costs and mileages, with the details assessed annually. One consequence of the agreement was the use of the Willebrew ticket system by East Yorkshire, and its retention long after the Setright had become widespread elsewhere - the clippings enabled the recording of fuller information than was otherwise readily practicable until after the development of sophisticated computer-based equipment many decades later.

The problem for the trams was that the best parts of the system, namely the outer sections on reserved track, were in the B area and they were accordingly abandoned on the same date. The routes were thus truncated at the very time when housing development meant that there could have been a case for their extension in the manner then current in cities such as Liverpool and Leeds. Nevertheless the real difficulties were probably financial and psychological, with loan repayments outstanding on the construction of the more recent sections, track renewals increasingly necessary elsewhere, and a widespread change of mood stifling the will to act in favour of tramway development.

Introduction of trolleybuses

A more positive approach was apparent when the Corporation began, also in 1934, to consider the possibilities of trolleybuses. It was decided to embark upon a programme in which the Hedon Road tramway would be converted to motorbus operation, and the other routes to trolleybuses, for which powers were granted in 1936. By this time Mr Morrison had moved (in 1935) to become manager at Bournemouth, where a similar programme of tram to trolleybus conversions was well advanced, and his successor in Hull was Mr J Lawson, who introduced the 'streamlined' livery in 1936. The proposed trolleybus routes were all within the city boundary and all within the A area as specified in the joint agreement with East Yorkshire.

Accordingly, the trolleybus system was formally inaugurated on 23rd July 1937 and the carriage of passengers began with service 61 two days later. Tram service S became trolleybus 62 later in the year, both these services operating via the unusually named Spring Bank, one of the main roads out of town. The conversions of tram service M (Hedon Road) to motorbuses and B to trolleybuses in 1938 were followed by the abandonment of service H (Holderness Road) early in 1940. This left only two tramway services, A and D, operating on track which increasingly gave cause for concern.

The city had invested in a total of 66 trolleybuses by 1940 for the operation of the four services 61-4 and their short workings. The motorbus fleet had also made further significant expansion by this date, partly for tram replacement as already noted, but also for services provided to recently built or hitherto unserved areas. The fleet of 110 at the end of 1935 had grown by a further 26% to 139 by the end of 1940, with an intake of 59 vehicles in this period. Again, the orders were shared between Daimler (35) and AEC (20), and four second-hand Leylands made up the balance. Overall, in the decade 1931-40 Daimler and AEC were the principal suppliers and were on almost equal terms, although Leyland was also significant. The first year of the new decade, 1941, was marked by the appointment of Mr G H Pulfrey, the innovative general manager who was to prove the longest-serving holder of this office with the Department; he retired in 1965.

The Second World War

The second world war was now dominating the nation's life. Enemy attacks naturally focussed first on London, the city hardest hit in the onslaught, and it is the blitz on the capital which still features most strongly in the nation's collective memory of the war. Hull, with its vast docks and industries facing Germany, and readily recognizable from the air, can lay claim to be on a tragic par with Coventry and Clydebank in the bombing of provincial cities. About 1,200 Hull citizens were directly killed in the bombing, only 3% of houses escaped damage, and some 152,000 people (half the city's population) were homeless at some time during the conflict. The Transport Department's Central Garage and Head Office, just over five years old, were completely destroyed on 7th May 1941, along with 44 motorbuses, which was one third of the fleet. At various times, the Department's other garages were also damaged, and of course the effect on the tram and trolleybus overhead was severe. Other operators came to the rescue at once, and about 40 buses were lent from various other parts of Yorkshire, mostly for short periods, and eight Daimlers were purchased from Wallasey. In consequence of the losses, the Ministry of Supply allocated significant numbers of new utility buses to Hull each year during the remainder of the war. These were 'unfrozen' AECs and Leylands in the first half of 1942 and Guy Arabs thereafter, totalling 50 wartime deliveries up to July 1945.

Unlike Coventry and Bristol, the raids did not cause the immediate end of the remaining tram routes, which were patched up for a while longer, but the track was in a very poor state. It proved possible to convert the Anlaby Road tramway to trolleybus operation in 1942, commencing on 6th September and using existing vehicles, and the best 32 of the trams were sold to Leeds. The last tram route, service D to Hessle Road (Dairycoates), had to wait until the arrival of twelve utility trolleybuses in June 1945. A decorated last tram, proudly displaying the city's three crowns, ran in ceremonial splendour on the last day of the month, and ten more of the cars were sold to Leeds, where they were unkindly known as 'kipper boxes'.

Hull's tram fleet was over 100 strong from 1904 to 1937; its maximum was 180 between 1925 and 1928. During its operational life the tramcar fleet contained a total of 181 cars, 25 of which had been built as trailer cars and later converted to be self-propelled. The last financial year in which trams were owned was that ending 31st March 1946 during which 18 cars were on the books.

Postwar redevelopment

A change of name now occurred for the Department, using the city's full title for the first time as Kingston upon Hull Corporation Transport. In the postwar years 1945-50 there was a boom in traffic, with a peak of 102 million passenger journeys made in 1948. A further 22 trolleybuses were delivered, bringing the fleet up to its maximum of 100, and the undertaking celebrated its golden jubilee in 1949. On the motorbus front, no fewer than 102 new AEC buses were purchased, including six single-deckers. Renewal on this scale had become a matter of urgency after wartime usage, damage and enforced neglect, but the five years to the end of 1950 also saw the motorbus fleet increased by almost 18% to a total of 152. These years saw the fleet standardized as never before, with 106 AEC Regents, 6 AEC Regals, 36 Guy Arabs and four Leyland TD7s.

As housing development continued, the trolleybuses were to prove successful in spite, or perhaps because, of their inability under the East Yorkshire agreement to be extended to new estates. The operation at high frequencies over densely populated routes was to obtain the best return from the investment in the fixed power supply equipment - for example, a two-minute headway was provided on the Hessle Road service.

One-man operation - a small start

After the huge postwar renewal of the fleet, the years 1951-9 saw only 16 new trolleybuses and 16 new motorbuses delivered. The latter included six stylish AEC Regents with the then-new enclosed radiator, but with a view to one-man operation there were ten two-door AEC Reliance single-deckers which introduced the

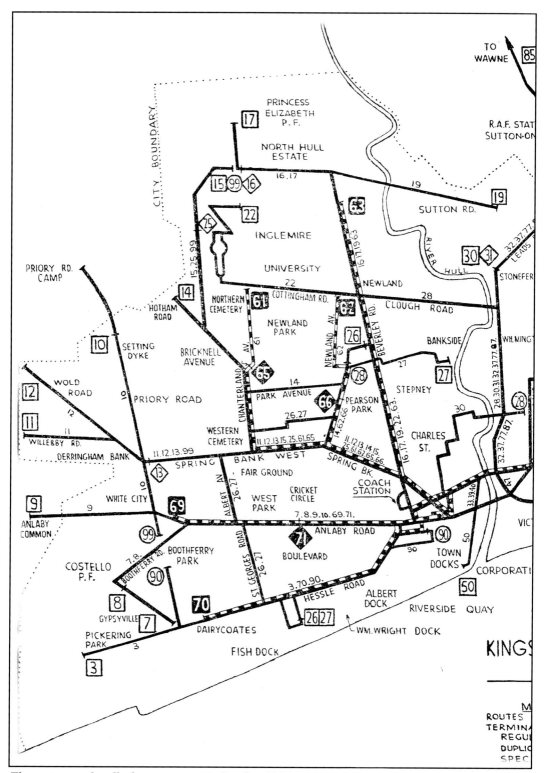

The motor- and trolleybus routes as at October 1955

In October 1955 this map was prepared for use in the undertaking's timetable. It shows a network of radial routes, those operated by trolleybuses being based very much on the earlier and by then long-abandoned tram routes. (Hull Local Studies Library)

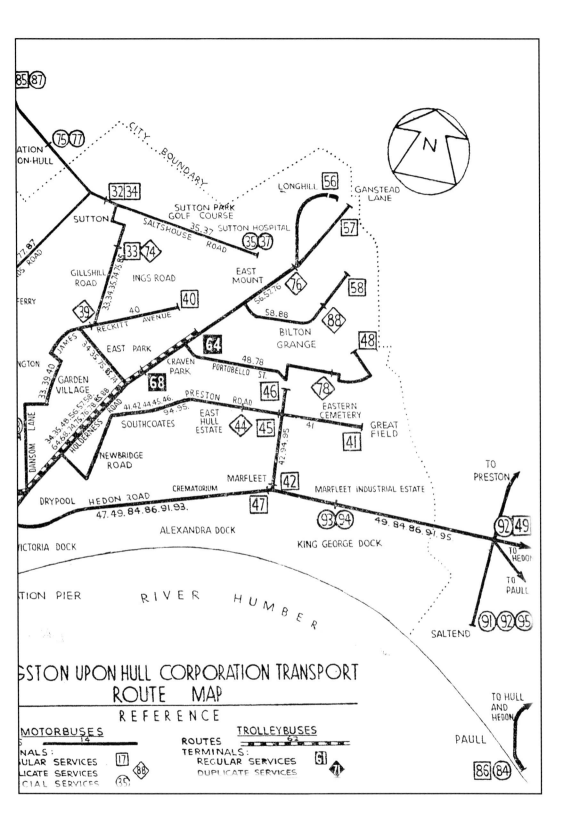

KINGSTON UPON HULL CORPORATION TRANSPORT
ROUTE MAP

REFERENCE

MOTORBUSES   TROLLEYBUSES
                             ROUTES
TERMINALS: TERMINALS:
REGULAR SERVICES   REGULAR SERVICES
DUPLICATE SERVICES   DUPLICATE SERVICES
SPECIAL SERVICES

HULL CORPORATION TROLLEYBUS SERVICES

Date commenced	Route numbers	Route	Last day of service
23rd July 1937	61	King Edward Street to Chanterlands Avenue North (Short workings 61A – later 65 - to Goddard Avenue)	28th July 1962
3rd October 1937	62	King Edward Street to Newland Avenue (Short workings 66 to Pearson Park)	16th November 1963
4th September 1938	63	King Edward Street to Beverley High Road/Endike Lane (Short depot workings 63A to Haworth Arms up to 1942)	31st October 1964
18th February 1940	64	Savile Street – later Jameson Street – to Holderness Road/Ings Road (Short workings 64A – later 68 – to East Park)	21st September 1963
1941	67	King Edward Street to Chanterlands Avenue via Beverley Road and Cottingham Road[1]	1943
6th September 1942	69	Waterworks Street[2] to Anlaby Road/Boothferry Road later Meadowbank Road (Short workings 71 to Boulevard)	3rd February 1962
1st July 1945	70	Waterworks Street[2] to Hessle Road	28th January 1961

[1] – Wartime service, believed to have operated during two separate periods in the years shown
[2] – In 1952 Waterworks Street was renamed as an extension of Paragon Street

underfloor engine to the fleet. The 16 trolleybuses were even more radical, with two staircases and doorways, the front door being ahead of the axle as on the revolutionary 1933 AEC Q. Hull's first two-door "Coronation" trolleybus, yet another distinctive number 101 in the fleet, also designed for one-man operation, was exhibited at the 1952 Commercial Motor Show and became nationally famous in the transport world. From today's perspective it is hard to realize how radical a change it was at the time. A production batch of 15 entered service in 1954/5 but agreement to operate them without a conductor was never reached in their lifetime.

Decline of the trolleybus

The circumstances favourable to the trolleybuses remained secure whilst housing clearance concentrated on the central areas where people would have been walking anyway rather than taking the bus, but as the demolition programme moved further out in the 1950s and 1960s, it began to undermine the foundation of the trolleybus system. Housing development in this period was dramatic, and many new or extended bus services were provided to the new estates, some jointly licensed with East Yorkshire in pursuance of the agreement. The 1959 decision to abandon the trolleybus system was a great shock in many quarters of the city, but it rested on the relationship between a network confined within the A area of the agreement and the prevailing pattern of housing development. There was intense controversy in and out of the council chamber, but the decision stood.

The years 1961-4 saw the closure of the trolleybus system, commencing with Hessle Road and ending with Beverley Road. The order of the closure programme was determined initially by the construction of flyover bridges on Hessle and Anlaby Roads, felt to be necessary as a way of circumventing the level crossing problem at a time of greatly increasing motor traffic. In this period a number of other level crossings were eliminated by railway closures under the Beeching programme which included the coastal lines from Hull to Hornsea and to Withernsea. As the trolleybus abandonment neared its end, much attention focussed on the Coronations, which could have been described as just nicely run in, but no buyer could be found other than the scrap man, although the electric motors saw further service in Bradford.

Fleet numbers had run from 1 to 116 on Hull trolleybuses, but there were never 116 in the fleet at the same time: the maximum was 100 from 1949 to 1953. In the days of that maximum the allocation was: Cottingham Road (C) 46; Holderness Road (H) 20; Liverpool Street (D) 18; Wheeler Street (A) 16. The apparently illogical letters for the last two related to "Dairycoates" and "Anlaby Road".

New Atlanteans and second-hand buses

Hull was an early user of the Leyland Atlantean rear-engined high-capacity double-decker, taking an initial batch of five in the summer of 1960. No-one could then have dreamed that the undertaking would go on to purchase 241 of this model, which in 1960 represented some 63% of the total number of motorbuses ever owned. The new regime was apparent as Atlanteans replaced trolleybuses on the first two conversions in 1961, but secondhand buses were used for the third. The ten ex-Newcastle Daimler CVG6 vehicles acquired in 1961, some twelve years after the last prewar Daimlers had been withdrawn, formed the first of several judicious purchases in the 1960s. The others were all AEC Regents, 19 of the RT-type from St Helens in 1962, 12 Regent IIIs from Leicester in 1966 and 36 from Nottingham in 1967. In the same period, the thrust towards one-man operation continued with the delivery of five more AEC Reliance 39-seaters in 1960 and twelve two-door Leyland Panthers in 1964-6. Meanwhile, most years after 1960 saw further deliveries of Leyland Atlanteans, all with Roe bodies. The first conversion of the type to one-man operation took place in September 1969 amid scepticism about the practicality of one-man operation of double-deckers on busy city services, but by this time the buses, always seen as a social service, were incurring heavy losses and, as with the trolleybuses ten years before, the decision stood. Many participants and observers would nevertheless see this event as the beginning of the end. An associated event in that year was the revision of the coordination agreement with East Yorkshire. This had the effect of merging the A and B areas and allowed both operators to adopt automated ticketing systems.

Consolidation of one-man operation

The permanence of the one-man venture was underlined by the delivery of most of a batch of 20 two-door Atlanteans before the end of the year, and the programme was pursued vigorously from then on. This type of operation was gaining ground everywhere under the prevailing economic imperatives, but at this juncture Hull took a commanding lead with its development of the Autofare system. Although this happened only just over 30 years ago, it was before the computer age, and the invention of a quick no-change system where every passenger got a ticket indicating the fare paid and stage boarded was an achievement of considerable ingenuity. The system was widely copied elsewhere. Its architect was the general manager Mr W K Haigh, hitherto deputy at Sunderland before he took over from Mr Pulfrey in 1965. Rapid progress was made on two fronts. First, the Hull system achieved the fastest boarding speeds for one-man operations anywhere, exceeding even Stevenage Superbus on which no tickets were issued, and being not much slower than buses with conductors. The operation was enthusiastically reported in Commercial Motor during 1972. Second, Hull was the first urban operator to achieve conversion of its whole network to one-man operation, which it did in November of that year when the last AEC Regent was withdrawn.

Demise of the streamlined livery

Two other changes occurred in 1972. A new livery was introduced, still blue and white but with much more white, and lacking the long-familiar and characteristic 'streamlining'; and the name of the undertaking was changed to Kingston upon Hull City Transport in anticipation of the abolition of corporations under the forthcoming changes to local government. This change of name reflected a much greater change for the city as a whole, neatly but pointedly summed up by one writer as follows: "In 1972 the Local Government Act inaugurated a profoundly controversial link-up of the north and south banks [of the Humber]. Hull lost its status as a county borough, which it had held since 1440, and was given the reduced status of a district authority in the new county of Humberside. It petitioned to retain its Lord Mayor but not its Sheriff and its wings were sharply clipped as it lost its control of such services as education and libraries, in which it had taken particular pride. Not surprisingly, it regarded Humberside as a usurper." (John Markham, *The Book of Hull*).

Later in the decade the Leyland supremacy in the fleet was challenged with the introduction of the sophisticated Scania-powered Metropolitan, followed in 1980/1 by the Gardner-powered Metrobus. A controversial innovation which was gaining ground at this time was the introduction of

coaches to municipal fleets, and a number of Leyland Leopard coaches was purchased in 1982/3. They carried a white livery trimmed in blue and maroon, displayed the fleetname Kingstonian, and operated a wide range of private hire, excursions, tours and express journeys. They were followed in 1984 by a Gardner-engined Leyland National adapted for wheelchairs and operating a weekly schedule of special routes for the disabled. This had the same livery as the coaches but bore the fleetname Handyrider rather than Kingstonian. In the main double-deck fleet, the final Leyland Atlanteans of 1982 were followed in 1984 by the first of a new type, the Dennis Dominator.

Deregulation

The outstanding event of the 1980s was the deregulation of bus services under the 1985 Transport Act. Put briefly, the change from public service to commercial enterprise was such an alien notion to the city and to the Transport Department that there was never any real hope that it could succeed. The city always determinedly took the view that the buses belonged to its people for the purpose of providing a social service, but the terms of the Act were opposed to this viewpoint and created strictures which crippled the traditional operations. This falling apart was neatly illustrated by the undertaking's timetables. For many years the KHCT comprehensive timetable booklet, designed to fit easily into pocket, handbag or sideboard drawer, was something of an institution. It usually had two editions a year, and showed times and fares for every service. Short workings, schools, works, or football journeys all had their own service numbers and were all included, and as a matter of principle all schools journeys within the city were worked by the municipal undertaking. The last booklet is believed to have been edition 77 in September 1983. From then on, as deregulation loomed, the dreaded leaflets appeared, accompanied by a miniature ring-binder in which to keep them. They were produced to a very high standard, but were no substitute for knowing that you had the up-to-date timetable for the whole system.

A new limited company

It became necessary to create a new company, Kingston upon Hull City Transport Limited, to operate the undertaking's services, and subsidies could no longer be apportioned from the rates. They had to be open to competitive tender, and as if to rub salt in the wound, whilst the City Council was (at arm's length) the operator, it was no longer they who granted the subsidies, but the Humberside County Council. Many school journeys in the city now went to small private operators, but conversely KHCT was sometimes the successful tenderer for schools in the rural hinterland.

The change was underlined by a complete renumbering of the city's services in July 1986, intended to mark the division between the old and the new undertaking, but in fact being a further unsettling influence just when stability was needed most. On the vehicle front, the most obvious effect of deregulation was the purchase of a fleet of minibuses, intended to penetrate housing areas unsuitable for full-size buses before competitors did the same. There had been a few (and unsuccessful) minibuses, on Ford A type chassis, but these later examples came in a dramatic new livery of maroon, a deliberate reversion to the colour of the trams, and were lined in gold and bore the fleetname "Royale". The name was chosen to reflect the King's Town of the city's origins, in a French form to underline the concept of Hull as "Gateway to Europe", a slogan of the world of modern marketing.

Financial struggles

In the five years after deregulation, KHCT Ltd struggled to maintain its position as the provider, albeit now commercially, of a social service, but its financial position worsened seriously until there was no option but to sell out. This course of action had some severe critics, who argued that the Council couldn't sell the buses because they weren't theirs to sell - they belonged to the people of Hull. With sympathy towards this viewpoint, the Council sought a sale to KHCT's own workforce, but was unable to negotiate it. The second preference was to sell to a company which itself belonged to its own employees, and this

time the Council was successful. The preferred bidder was Cleveland Transit Ltd and the purchase was completed in December 1993.

This really was the end. The fact that the undertaking did not at this time change its name was not the point. The really significant thing was symbolic - the buses, like the trolleybuses and trams before them, had always proudly displayed the three crowns of the city's ancient coat of arms, and this, the sign of belonging to the city, was now removed from the fleet. The address shown on the buses ceased to be Lombard Street, Kingston upon Hull, and became Church Road, Stockton on Tees. The notion of the buses belonging, through their workforce, to the people of the city was finally extinguished a year later when Cleveland Transit sold out to Stagecoach Holdings. For the buses it was small consolation when, after much vociferous campaigning, Humberside County Council was abolished in 1996, an East Riding of Yorkshire county authority was re-created, and Hull regained its county borough status, albeit expressed in strange new language as a 'unitary authority'.

The heritage

It will not have escaped your attention that Hull has repeatedly been a pioneer in the development of its transport services. It was no less a pioneer in the museum world, and established Britain's first municipal transport museum in 1936. Now greatly enhanced and in new premises, this is well worth a visit. Its treasures include Britain's oldest surviving tram (Ryde Pier car, 1871), the great rarity of a steam tram locomotive (Portstewart), Hull's own tramcar No. 132 and AEC Regent bus No. 328.

Acknowledgements

In the pages that follow, you can browse through the events of the years, and the story told here in words will unfold before you in pictures. The telling of this story owes much to the following writers:

Buckley, Richard:
   Hull's Steam Tramway, Tramway
   Review 83/4, Autumn/Winter 1975;

Horse Tramways in Hull, *Tramway Review 111/2, Autumn/Winter 1982.*

Goldspink, H C:
Various papers published in Buses Illustrated and by The Omnibus Society and others deposited in Hull's Local Studies library.

Graystone, Philip:
The Blitz on Hull, *1991.*

Markham, John:
The Book of Hull, *1989.*

Nicholson, J S:
The Tramways of Kingston upon Hull, *Trams Nos 27-29, 1967-8.*

O'Connell, G M:
British Bus & Tram Systems, 19 - Hull Corporation, *in Buses Illustrated 31/2, May/June and July/August 1957;*
British Trolleybus Systems, 17 - Kingston upon Hull, *Buses 215/7, Feb & April 1973;*
KHCT 1899-1979, *An Illustrated History of Kingston upon Hull City Transport, 1979.*

The PSV Circle:
Fleet History PB22, Kingston upon Hull City Transport.

Wells, Malcolm:
Kingston upon Hull Trolleybuses, *1996*

Even with the aid of those excellent publications, this book would have been a poorer work without the help the writer has received from friends Philip Battersby and Ron Maybray, whose constant, ungrudgingly given support in the writer's endeavours cannot be overestimated and is yet again humbly acknowledged.

Access to microfilmed copies of *The Hull Daily Mail* as well as a number of historic photographs were provided by that newspaper's Editor and the staff of its Library. My visit to the paper's splendid new offices on the site of what I recall from my youth as a derelict paint factory was a highlight in the preparation of this book.

Research assistance by staff of the Local Studies unit of Hull's Central Library was similarly efficiently and cheerfully given: access to microfilms of *The Hull Times* and to a wide variety of other documents provided many useful details and confirmed others.

Mr Malcolm Taylor of the Hull City Archives provided confirmatory details from the Public Transport Committee minutes of the disastrous fires in 1978 and 1979.

Tireless proofreaders David and Mary Shaw have once again applied their patent gremlin-chasing skills to the text, to its undoubted benefit.

Photographic sources are as named in the captions, with particular thanks to David Packer, who is now the custodian of some of the late L R Storry's Hull negatives.

In other words, it is demonstrated once again that an author produces a work by building upon the earlier work and present help of a large number of people - all he can do is offer grateful thanks and hope that his work will add something to what has gone before. With all that expert help behind him, the writer ought to have produced a work free from errors: if any have slipped through they are his responsibility alone.

As always with this series of books, a *caveat*: it is stressed that neither a definitive history nor a detailed fleet list is being offered. Rather is the book intended to be a visual journey through the years, charting Hull's public transport as it expanded successfully and then declined to a state in which the only cure was to sell it off. As is usual with such journeys - especially one confined to 104 pages - not everything can be examined or even mentioned; and if, for example, Newland Avenue, Beverley Road, Botanic Gardens and Spring Bank West seem to receive a lot of attention, well: they were the areas in which I lived and went to school. The photographs speak for themselves: I have tried to leave in lots of background and can only regret that some subjects seem never to have been photographed.

John Banks
Romiley, Cheshire
July 2003

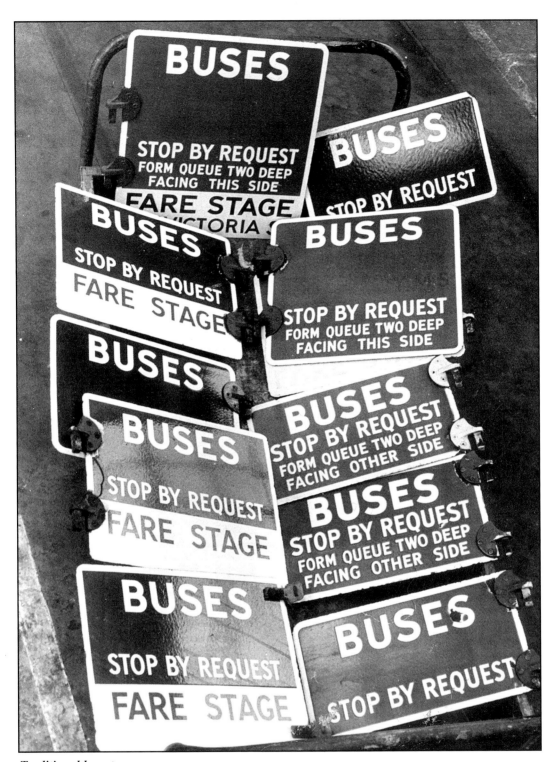

Traditional bus stops
There were celebrations at the demise of the tramcars and then of the trolleybuses: why not for the old bus stops one had known for decades? Hull's, like those everywhere else, were deemed inadequate and were replaced by "Euro" signs of a sort to be found in all Common Market countries. The local paper had the fine idea of recording a barrow-load before they disappeared. *(Hull Daily Mail)*

Part One - Horse Power and Electric Trams

It is never easy to find illustrations of early vehicles in towns and cities other than London and in the case of Hull such material has proved particularly scarce. This picture of a horse bus, therefore, was an interesting find. The writer admits to knowing little about it other than what can be gleaned from the picture: it advertised a route between Spring Bank and Victoria Pier at a fare of one penny. The driver in his tall shiny hat and uncompromising black garb must have been rather warm in the bright sunshine and surely that is Stan Laurel looking over the back of the top deck? *(Hull Daily Mail)*

Hull Street Tramways

Above: Car No. **15** on the route between Victoria Pier and Beverley Road. The photograph was taken at the junction of Queens Road and Beverley Road. *(John Banks Collection)*

Below: Car No. **23** entering the depot in Stepney Lane for the last time, on 30th September 1899. The placards on the sides of the car read "Ring out the Old, Ring in the New" and a valedictory flag waves above the destination board. *(Hull Daily Mail)*.

The Drypool and Marfleet Steam Tramway Company

Above: The Company, which ran from the outer side of North Bridge and along Hedon Road, operated steam locomotives hauling 74-seat, double-deck trailer cars for about a dozen years between 1889 and January 1901. It had a fleet of eight Kitson locomotives, of which this is No. **4**. There were also eight trailer cars. *(John Banks Collection)*

Below: Advertising has increased considerably, with Nestlé's Milk prominent, but local traders extolling fireplaces (King & Company) and pianos (Holders) are also conspicuous. Holder Brothers was a well-known name for all matters musical in the city for decades: the writer recalls buying 78rpm records from their shop in the 1950s. *(John Banks Collection)*

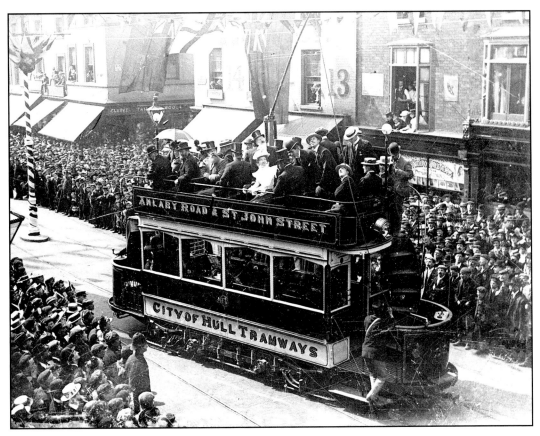

The first electric tramcars

Above: Car No. **25**, a Milnes 51-seater, at the formal opening of the system on 5th July 1899. Vast crowds have turned out and most windows have their quota of onlookers. *(Hull Daily Mail)*

Below: Probably also on inauguration day, a similar car is seen at the Wheeler Street terminus of the Anlaby Road service. *(Tramway & Railway World)*

Above: Holderness Road (H) depot opened in 1903 and this picture is believed to date from about that time. Tramcar No. **58** is ready to go out on the "H" route. New in 1900, it was a Brush 51-seater, one of a batch of 30. Nineteen-hundred was a remarkable year for new trams, with 61 delivered. *(John Banks Collection)*

Below: Car No. 84, a 1900 Milnes, was built as an open-topped trailer car and was quickly motorised and fitted with a top cover. Driver George Turner looks suitably proud of his charge as it waits to return to town from Newland Avenue on the "S" Spring Bank route. His conductor, visible upstairs, was killed in the First World War. *(Reproduced by courtesy of Mrs Enid Turner)*

>> *Opposite page upper:* Covered-top car No. **33** at the ferry terminus of the "P" Pier route. This was the first tram route to be abandoned, on 5th September 1931. *(Hull Daily Mail)*

>> *Opposite page lower:* The model of the experimental tram No. **101** built in the Hull Corporation workshops in 1923 for display at the British Empire Exhibition at Wembley in 1924. The model still exists and can be seen in the Hull Streetlife Museum. *(Hull Daily Mail)*

31

Hull's tram fleet was large, fascinating and complicated and it would not have been difficult to fill all the pages of this book with pictures of it. To round off our coverage, here are two views of what might be described as "trams in the landscape". In the King Edward Street scene *(above)* a number of cars, led by Milnes No. **79**, one of the former trailer cars, on the "S" Spring Bank route, show the moveable top covers with which many of the open-topped cars were fitted in the period 1903-5. These covers had windows that could be fully lowered and the roof panels could be raised after the manner of a roll-top desk; they required so much time and effort for their frequent adjustment that the fitting of fixed top covers commenced in 1905, although it was some years before all the moveable roofs were replaced. The view *(below)* of Cottingham Road at the junction of Beverley Road, outside the Haworth Arms public house, is one of the few that show tram and motor-bus public transport side by side. Both car No. **145**, a 1912 Brush fully enclosed 62-seater, on the short-working (of the "B" route) "BN" to Beverley Road (Haworth Arms) and 1932 AEC Regent No. **73** (**RH 4761**) were heading for the town centre. The bus, a Brush-bodied 46-seater, was on route 21 from Hall Road (Inglemire Lane), which replaced the "BC" trams and had run via Chanterlands Avenue until 29th July 1934: the picture is thus later than that date. *(Ron Maybray Collection; L R Storry)*

Part Two - The Trolleybuses

Leylands 1-26

The 26 Leyland TB2s were delivered in 1937 as 54-seaters, bodied by the Surrey coachbuilders Weymann's at the latter's Addlestone factory, and were reseated to 56 just after the war. They lasted in service until 1952-5. Number **1** (**CRH 925**) is seen when brand new and before entering service *(right)*. The original livery layout proudly incorporated the name of the city on the upper deck panels and the destination blinds were of the less-usual black-on-white

type. The use of the word "City" to denote the inward destination did not, in the writer's recollection, accord with the universal use by Hull's citizens of the word "town" for that location.

Below: Number **2** (**CRH 926**) was turning in Queen Victoria Square soon after inauguration of the first route, the 61. Chanterlands Avenue North was abbreviated to "Chants Av North" on the blinds and it is recalled that the English master at school once chastised a pupil for using the expression "down Chants" in answer to the question "where do you live?". Teacher was right, of course, but everyone said it... *(John Banks Collection; Hull Daily Mail)*

<< *Opposite page:* The second trolleybus route to be started using the Leyland TB2s was the 62 from King Edward Street to Newland Avenue, inaugurated on 3rd October 1937. In a fine view of the City Hall *(upper)* No. **25** (**CRH 949**) is negotiating Queen Victoria Square between inward and outward journeys. On the same day *(lower)* No. **26** (**CRH 950**) was being used for driver familiarisation with "RESERVED" in the front destination screen. Apart from the trolleybuses, there are many other fascinating aspects to these pictures, not least the prominent cast streetname sign that proves the identity of "Queen Victoria Square". The word "Queen" was, and is, often omitted in both speech and writing. *(Both: John Banks Collection)*

Upper: In this view of No. **22** (**CRH 946**) in Cottingham Road, having just come off the 62, the livery has been modified to exclude "HULL" on the upper-deck panels. The guard rail is painted white and one headlight is masked, suggesting an early wartime photograph. The large route numbers were to aid readability for intending passengers in the blackout. *(The Omnibus Society)*

Centre: Anlaby Road on 10th April 1954. Just out of view was a railway level crossing, no doubt the cause of the traffic jam on this occasion. Leyland No. **18** (**CRH 942**) on the 69 is becalmed ahead of two AEC Regents and another trolleybus. Number 18 was withdrawn in 1955. *(L R Storry)*

Lower: In Cottingham Road depot on 23rd March 1952, No. **3** (**CRH 927**) heads a line of trolleybuses waiting to go out on service. Cottingham Road (C) depot was the second largest and had been used by trams until 1938. *(L R Storry)*

Crossleys 27-46

<< **Opposite page upper:** Hull's third trolleybus route was opened on 4th September 1938 and ran from King Edward Street to the junction of Beverley High Road and Endike Lane. For this expansion the department ordered a batch of 20 Crossley TDD7 chassis with Cravens 54-seat bodywork, of which No. **37** (**ERH 37**) is seen on inauguration day. The first of the Crossleys to be withdrawn went in 1954, but No. 37 was one of the last to go, in 1962. *(Hull Daily Mail)*

<< **Opposite page lower:** A rare image of the wartime all-over blue livery. Crossley No. **28** (**ERH 28**) was turning at the end of the 62 route: the U-turn was performed across Cottingham Road and was very tight. The wires going off along Cottingham Road were little used in passenger service, but were essential for Chanterlands Avenue trolleybuses travelling to and from Cottingham Road depot. *(The Omnibus Society)*

Upper: Number **40** (**ERH 40**) in 1961 at the King Edward Street starting point for service 61 to Chanterlands Avenue North. Visible behind the vehicle is the inspectors' hut from which departures were controlled. *(John Banks)*

Lower: The last service 70 trolleybus from Paragon Street to Dairycoates ran on 28th January 1961 and was operated by Crossley No. 29. A fortnight earlier, sister vehicle No. **28** (**ERH 28**) was on the route. This view shows the three crowns of the coat of arms well, not to mention the carelessly set destination blind. *(Hull Daily Mail)*

Leylands 47-66

Above: For the opening of the Holderness Road route 64 on 18th February 1940 Hull returned to Leyland Motors for 20 TB7 chassis. The coachbuilder was again changed, and the order for bodywork went to East Lancashire Coachbuilders, of Blackburn. The completed vehicles were delivered between August 1939 and February 1940. The appearance of vehicles across three batches from different bodybuilders varied remarkably little. Number **51** (**FRH 551**) was brand new. *(East Lancashire Coachbuilders)*

Below: Leyland TB7 No. **53** (**FRH 553**) receives attention from the signwriter. For many years advertisements were not carried on Hull Corporation vehicles. When they were finally accepted in 1951 to generate additional revenue, they were signwritten rather than pasted paper. *(A D Packer Collection/L R Storry)*

Above: Number **51** (**FRH 551**) again, this time in a picture dating from 16th September 1956. It had just left the 64 terminus in Jameson Street and is crossing the junction with King Edward Street (on the left) and Prospect Street. Two East Yorkshire Leyland PD2 Titans and a Corporation AEC Regent follow. *(A D Packer Collection/L R Storry)*

Below: The Leyland TB7s were withdrawn between 1957 and 1961. Number **55** (**FRH 555**) was one of the last to go and it is seen here in Paragon Square, outside the Royal Station Hotel and the railway station, setting down passengers at the end of its inward run from Holderness Road. It will turn right into Jameson Street to gain the departure stand for its next outward run. These arrangements using Paragon Square were altered on 22nd March 1959, so the photograph is before that date. *(Geoffrey Holt)*

Sunbeams 67-78

The 66-strong Hull trolleybus fleet, on the outbreak of war in September 1939, was modern and there were enough vehicles to allow the opening, on 6th September 1942, of another route, the 69 from Waterworks Street to Anlaby Road. On the following day service 67 from King Edward Street to Chanterlands Avenue North via Beverley Road and Cottingham Road was started. This was one of the rare occasions when the Cottingham Road wiring between Newland Avenue and Chanterlands Avenue North was used for service running as opposed to dead mileage to and from Cottingham Road depot. One wonders why the 67 and the 61 were never joined as a circular.

Above: The next new trolleybuses arrived in June 1945 and were a batch of twelve based on the Sunbeam W model - a utility chassis built to a specification laid down by the Ministry of Supply with vehicles being allocated by the Ministry of War Transport - with Brush 56-seat bodywork. The latter was also built to a utility specification that had originally called for a very angular outline, lacking in curves and devoid of anything even approaching luxury: strictures that were slightly relaxed towards and just after the end of the war. These twelve vehicles were withdrawn in 1962/3. Inside Liverpool Street depot in the 1950s, the two vehicles on the left are from this batch: Nos **70/8** (**GRH 290/8**). On the right are Leyland TB2s Nos **14/8** (**CRH 938/42**). *(A D Packer Collection/L R Storry)*

Below: Number **74** (**GRH 294**) on the rarely illustrated 71 short working (of the 69) to Boulevard. The vehicle is turning out of Boulevard into Anlaby Road and has just turned on the Malm Street reverser: in the background another trolleybus can be seen reversing into Malm Street. *(R F Mack)*

Above: Rear views of trolleybuses, especially those with utility bodywork, are not common. This one is of No. **68** (**GRH 288**) pulling away from the 63 stand in Jameson Street in 1961. *(John Banks)*

Below: An activity inseparable from bus operation is keeping them clean. The atmosphere in industrial cities can very quickly dull and corrode paintwork. Hull's livery, with its broad expanses of white swoops and whirls, was more likely than most to suffer and it was immaculately kept. Daily washing in Cottingham Road depot is illustrated as No. **77** (**GRH 297**) passes through the mechanical washer. An AEC Regent and another trolleybus wait their turn and vehicles already dealt with are parked on the left awaiting their next duty. *(A D Packer Collection/L R Storry)*

Sunbeams 79-84

Above: A further six Sunbeam Ws with relaxed utility bodywork came in late 1945 and early 1946. This time the bodies were built by Charles Roe, of Crossgates, Leeds. As with the Brush version, the Roe bodywork had 56 seats. Number **79** (**GRH 355**) is shown at the outer terminus of the Hessle Road 70 route. *(R F Mack)*

Below: Numbers **83** and **84** (**GRH 359/60**) are seen on the Witham approach to North Bridge on 21st September 1963. This was the last day of trolleybuses on the Holderness Road 64 route. *(A D Packer Collection/L R Storry)*

Sunbeams 85-90

Above: The Sunbeam W - a wartime chassis - lingered into the postwar period, and in 1947 Hull received six more, which remained in service until withdrawal and scrapping in 1963. The Roe bodywork now had 60 seats. Number **85** (**HRH 85**) is seen turning out of South Street onto the Jameson Street 64 stand - arrangements that came into force in 1959 *(see page 39)*. *(L R Storry)*

Below: Number **86** (**HRH 86**) at the Newland Avenue terminus of the 62 route in 1961. *(Geoffrey Holt)*

Sunbeams 91-100

<< Opposite page: Ten Sunbeam S4s, delivered in June 1948, had Roe 60-seat bodywork and were eight feet wide. All ten were withdrawn and scrapped in 1963. On the opposite page *(upper)* No. **94** (**HRH 94**) contrasts its extra width with 7ft 6ins-wide No. **85** (**HRH 85**) in South Street on 7th April 1962. Number **98** (**HRH 98**) *(lower)* was at Princes Avenue junction with Queens Road on 2nd October 1963. The 62 route was withdrawn on 16th November. *(L R Storry; John C Gillham)*

Above: Two of the eight-footers, Nos **94/100** (**HRH 94/100**), and an earlier Sunbeam, utility No. **83** (**GRH 359**), are seen on 6th November 1960 in Carr Lane at a temporary terminus. It is believed that the cause was a major traffic light installation at Queen Victoria Square. With neither turning circle nor reverser at this point, the job of reversing the direction of an intensively worked trolleybus service cannot have been easy. *(A D Packer Collection/L R Storry)*

Right: Even when there *were* reversing facilities, there were often problems, as when No. **99** (**HRH 99**) became dewired at the Malm Street reverser in Boulevard. The trolleybus was on the 71 - a short working of the 69 Anlaby Road route - and had been reversing to take up the return run to town. Help had arrived in a Karrier tower wagon. *(A D Packer Collection/L R Storry)*

The "Coronation" Sunbeams 101-16

Above: The 1953 prototype "Coronation" trolleybus, No. 101 *(see page 10)*, was successful and a further 15 were ordered for 1954/5 delivery. In most respects they were the same as No. 101. They never ran as intended in driver-only operation and upon final abandonment of the trolleybus system in 1964 they were sold for scrap when barely ten years old. Number **111** (**RKH 111**) was in Queen Victoria Square in April 1956. *(John Banks Collection/G H F Atkins)*

Below: Number **102** (**RKH 102**) was exhibited at the 1954 Commercial Motor Show. Here it is on Beverley Road on 2nd October 1963. *(John C Gillham)*

Above: Referring again to the picture of No. 101 on page 10, here is a view of the arrival side of the 63 route terminus, with Endike Lane on the left. Number **107** (**RKH 107**) shows the interesting rear aspect of the Coronations, in particular the built-in trolley retrievers, which did away with the long, cumbersome bamboo poles used on earlier types. *(Ribble Enthusiasts Club)*

Below: On 31st October 1964, the 63 Beverley Road route, the last remaining, ran for the last time. On the fateful day, No. **108** (**RKH 108**) and its crew mark the occasion at the entrance to Cottingham Road depot. *(L R Storry)*

Trolleybuses in difficulties or when the going was tough...

...around the streets of Hull always caught the attention of the youthful enthusiast and, occasionally, that of somebody with a camera: in the fifties the latter would more often than not be Les Storry.

Above left: Sunbeam W No. **81** (**GRH 357**), disabled, is overtaken by Coronation No. **104** (**RKH 104**) on Chanterlands Avenue. *(L R Storry)*

Centre left: Sunbeam W No. **71** (**GRH 291**) with conductor using the notorious bamboo pole. The trolleybus was at the outer terminus of the 61, but facing town; perhaps it was out of service with a defect and had been replaced by overtaking Crossley No. **45** (**ERH 45**). *(L R Storry)*

Below left: Two Crossleys - No. **33** (**ERH 33**) heading towards the camera - in the snow at Botanic Gardens on 25th February 1958. *(A D Packer Collection/L R Storry)*

>> *Opposite page upper:* 1947 Sunbeam W No. **89** (**HRH 89**) heads a line of trolleybuses in George Street, on the approach to North Bridge, all stranded by a power failure in September 1961. *(Hull Daily Mail)*

>> *Opposite page lower left:* Crossley No. **34** (**ERH 34**) with trolley pole trouble on 10th July 1957 at Chanterlands Avenue North. *(L R Storry)*

>> *Opposite page lower right:* Crossley No. **32** (**ERH 32**) in an April 1958 thunderstorm in King Edward Street; the date was the 15th - Budget Day - and perhaps the gloom was understandable. *(Hull Daily Mail)*

Part Three - Prewar Motorbuses

Above: In the first decade of the last century residents of Wilmington and Stoneferry campaigned for a public transport service and some tram tracks were laid. A change of plan saw six second-hand Saurer 34-seat open-top motorbuses acquired and on 29th July 1909 (another source says 31st July) a service was started from New Cleveland Street, near North Bridge, to Stoneferry Green. The service was not entirely successful and ceased operation on 5th April 1912; the buses were withdrawn from stock in 1913. They had been new in 1905 to, but never used by, the Mersey Railway Company, Birkenhead, and had bodywork by Brown & Hughes. One of them is seen at Stoneferry Green, probably in the first few weeks of the service. *(Hull Daily Mail)*

Left: Three AECs were bought in 1921: one single- and two double-deckers. The single-decker was No. **1** (**AT 2934**), a K-type chassis with 33-seat, rear-entrance bodywork. It was used as a committee coach; in this view with Skidby Mill in the background, it had perhaps taken the august members out to lunch. The vehicle was scrapped in 1932. *(John Banks Collection)*

Above: In 1923 the business of the Hessle and District Motor Company, also known as the Blue Bus Company, was taken over by Hull Corporation. It is not known whether this solid-tyred, open-topped bus - believed to have been manufactured by Dennis Bros, of Guildford - passed into the Hull fleet. *(John Banks Collection)*

Right: New vehicles in 1923 were a single-deck Guy 26-seat saloon and nine open-top, outside-staircase double-deckers on the Bristol 4-ton chassis. Bodywork was by English Electric and had 53 seats: a high capacity for those days; it looks as though there may have been seats for 30 on the top deck and doubtless passengers were rather cramped. This one is No. **4** (**AT 7353**), the first of them. All nine were withdrawn in 1931/2 and most passed to the dealer Autowreckers, who in the writer's childhood had Aladdin's Cave-type premises in Clough Road. *(Ron Maybray Collection)*

Above: Hull's first covered-top bus was this AEC 409, with bodywork by Short Brothers, of Rochester, variously described as a 48- or 54-seater. Number **14** (**KH 3425**) was new in 1926 and after a short life, even by the standards of the time, was scrapped by Autowreckers in 1932. *(John Banks Collection)*

Below: Pneumatic tyres first appeared on Hull double-deck buses on some 1927/8 Bristol A types, typified by No. **42** (**KH 6239**), seen here when brand new. The 56-seat bodywork, by Charles Roe, also had the luxury of an enclosed platform and staircase. *(Senior Transport Archive)*

Above: Another of the 1928 Bristol As, regrettably unidentifiable, photographed outside Hammond's department store in Paragon Square at the departure stand for the New Bridge Road service, situated at that location from 1923 to 1935. *(John Banks Collection)*

Below: In anticipation of the granting of trolleybus running powers, twelve six-wheeled trolleybuses were ordered for 1930 delivery from Guy Motors, of Wolverhampton. In the event the powers were not granted and the order was changed to one for twelve motorbuses similar to several already in the fleet. One of those earlier vehicles, No. **52** (**RH 8455**), a 1929 Guy FCX with Brush 59-seat bodywork, is also seen on the New Bridge Road route at the terminus in Preston Road. *(John Banks Collection)*

The magnificent Guy six-wheelers, in the full panoply of the maroon and cream livery with the three crowns coat of arms and fully lined out in gold, must have been an awe-inspiring sight as they trundled majestically along the city's streets, many of them narrow. Above is another view of No. **52** (**KH 8455**), this time when the vehicle was brand new. Also brand new *(below)* was No. **61** (**RH 1284**), again bodied by Brush, but as a 62-seater. This vehicle dated from 1930 and was one of those that had been ordered as trolleybuses. Six of those twelve were bodied by Brush and six by Roe. *(Both: John Banks Collection)*

And here *are* the Guys in the city's streets... In the remarkable picture above, taken outside East Hull Baths on Holderness Road, one of the 1929 Brush-bodied 59-seaters, No. **48** (**KH 8451**), is heading for Jameson Street on the 46 from New Bridge Road. Before 1930 bus routes were identified by a system of plates and coloured lights. That became illegal in 1930 and routes were given numbers. Going the other way is No. **58** (**RH 1216**) of 1930. This was another of the Guys ordered as trolleybuses and was one of the six bodied by Roe as 64-seaters. In this picture it was heading for Preston Road via New Bridge Road. The view below is of another of the 1930 Roe-bodied machines, its identity masked by the driver and conductor standing in front of the radiator. It was in Paragon Street, with the Tivoli Theatre and Paragon Square in the background, waiting to depart for Boothferry Road. *(Both: Hull Daily Mail)*

Above: Never very common in the Hull fleet until the 1980s, the Dennis chassis appeared in 1931 in the shape of four HV models carrying Ransomes 51-seat bodywork. The batch is represented by No. **69** (**RH 3234**), photographed when brand new. The four were all withdrawn in 1938 and went on to have an unusual second career as mobile mortuaries with the Ministry of Health, for which work their tops were removed. *(John Banks Collection)*

Below: The department borrowed two Daimler CH6 double-deckers from the Daimler Motor Company Ltd in 1931, and purchased them in 1934. Illustrated is No. **101** (**VC 9980**), which was bodied by Brush as a 54-seater: the other, No. 98, had a 52-seat body by Charles Roberts. *(John Banks Collection)*

>> *Opposite page:* In 1931 Mr D P Morrison, who had been in charge at Dundee for five years, came to Hull as the new General Manager. One of his first acts was to repaint the motorbus fleet blue and white: a livery he had left behind him at Dundee. In 1932 orders were placed for AEC Regals and

Regents, variously bodied by Brush and English Electric. There were ten Regals, five bodied by each coachbuilder, with 28-seats and two doors: the typically Scottish rear platform was for boarding only and passengers left the bus via the front exit. In 1938 the front exits were removed and the seating capacity increased to 31. Our views are of No. **5** (**RH 4755**), one of the Brush examples. Three of the Regals were destroyed by bombing in 1941: the rest, including No. 5, were withdrawn in 1949. *(All: John Banks Collection)*

Above: The five 1932 AEC Regals, Nos 6-10, that were bodied by English Electric are represented by No. **10** (**RH 4760**). No attempt had been made to produce identical designs and the two batches of five were easily told apart through the many detail differences between the two coachbuilders' products, the most pronounced being the depth of the rain guttering over the side windows, the proportions of the driver's door windows and the number of bars on the guard rails.

Below: This unique illustration - at least, it is the only one known to the writer - shows one (unfortunately it is not known which) of the 1932 Brush-bodied AEC Regals after the 1938 conversion work that resulted in them becoming single-doorway 31-seaters. The picture was taken at Central Garage, Lombard Street. (*English Electric; Ron Maybray Collection*)

Above: From the 1932 intake of 20 AEC Regents we illustrate three of the ten bodied as 57-seaters by English Electric: from left to right Nos **87**, **86** and **88** (**RH 4775/4/6**). With these buses, and the same year's single-deckers, the shape and layout of the typical Hull bus that was to remain with little change, apart from minor ones to dimensions as regulations were painfully slowly modernised, for the next 30 years or so, was established. *(English Electric)*

Below: In 1934 a batch of 20 Daimler CP6 double-deckers arrived. Again the bodywork order was split, with ten each being supplied by English Electric and Weymann. That illustrated is No. **109** (**RH 6117**), an English Electric example. Seven of this sub-batch were lost to German bombing in 1941. *(English Electric)*

Above: At the height of the blitz during the Second World War, London Transport lost so many vehicles to enemy bombing that a call for help went out to provincial operators for the loan of buses. Hull Corporation sent eleven of the 1932 AEC Regents, and one of them is seen in the Capital in 1940. Number **91** (**RH 4779**) was on London's route 2 alongside a similar vehicle that had been lent by Leeds Corporation. The Hull buses were in London from October to December 1940, going thence on loan to Sheffield Corporation until May 1941. Seven of the twenty 1932 AEC Regents were lost in the 1941 air raids. *(Ron Maybray Collection)*

Below: The revolutionary side-engined AEC Q type was tried by a number of operators but was not destined to be successful. Hull took one, No. **127** (**RH 7747**), in 1933. Also lent to London in 1941, it was withdrawn in 1944. *(John Banks Collection)*

Above: Along with the four Dennis HVs ordered for delivery in 1931 *(see page 56)*, the department decided to sample the Titan TD1, a recently introduced model designed by G J Rackham of Leyland Motors. A batch of four was supplied, with Leyland bodywork seating 51. This one is No. **66** (**RH 3239**), photographed in April 1931 before delivery to Hull. *(John Banks Collection)*

Below: The Titans were well received and the department entered into negotiations with Leyland Motors for the loan of another four. Number **93** (**TF 6821**) was one of them, borrowed for six months from November 1931. It was not kept, was returned to Leyland and ended up in the Cardiff Corporation fleet. *(John Banks Collection)*

In 1932 a further twelve Leyland Titans were borrowed from the maker and were purchased in 1934. The main picture shows No. **103** (**TF 7862**) on route 39 to Garden Village at Queen Victoria Square in June 1932; the lady pedestrian was doubtless cursed by the photographer. The inset is of No. **115** (**TF 7220**) in as-built condition in December 1931. (*John Banks Collection*)

Hull's General Manager, Mr Morrison, moved in 1935 to become manager at Bournemouth, and his successor in Hull was Mr J Lawson, who introduced the streamlined livery in 1936. The first vehicles to carry the new livery were a batch of 20 Daimler COG5 56-seaters with bodywork by Weymann. Their registration numbers were CAT 151-70 - three-letter marks had been introduced by Hull CBC in June 1934. In 1937 a further 15 similar Weymann-bodied Daimlers came and were allocated registration numbers DKH 11-25.

Upper: Number **169** (**CAT 170**) of the 1936 batch is seen during the war or very soon after it. The bus has a white marking on the front mudguard - one of several measures designed to make vehicles more visible in the blackout. Note the oddly matched headlamps: the smaller on the offside was of a type fitted during the war. (*The Omnibus Society*)

Centre: An earlier picture shows No. **153** (**CAT 154**) in Paragon coach station on service 15. The livery above the lower-deck windows is more elaborate than it would become: compare with No. 169 above. (*W J Haynes*)

Lower: Number **16** (**DKH 16**) was from the 1937 batch and is seen in rural surroundings. The vehicles illustrated on this page were withdrawn in 1949, 1948 and 1949 respectively. The body from No. 16 was one of the few from this batch not to be reused in the programme to rebody wartime AEC Regents and Guy Arabs and the complete vehicle was sold to a new owner upon withdrawal. (*A D Packer Collection/L R Storry*)

Upper: In 1939 the department returned to the Associated Equipment Company, of Southall, for a batch of 20 AEC Regents. These vehicles were fairly unusual in being fitted with Gardner engines. The order for the 56-seat bodywork went to Massey Brothers, of Wigan. The batch, registered FRH 570-89, was delivered to Hull between October 1939 and January 1940 and thus all entered service after war had begun. Number **172** (**FRH 572**) appears in a picture doubly rare and unusual: it is a unique rear view of one of these buses and it shows the all-over blue livery. The vast canopy over the coach station platforms is in the background. *(The Omnibus Society)*

Centre: The first of the batch, No. **170** (**FRH 570**), is standing in more or less the same place in the coach station in the late 1940s; it was withdrawn in 1949. *(R F Mack)*

Lower: The bodies from 13 of these 1939 Regents were reused: those from Nos 170 and 172 on 1942 AEC Regents Nos 191 and 193. The worn out wartime bodywork was mounted on the donor chassis for disposal. The former No. 171 (**FRH 571**), having donated its body to another wartime Regent, No. 192, then gained a utility body in the manner described. These 1939 chassis with time-expired wartime bodies never ran in public service and many became lorries for new owners. Number 171, however, became a showman's van and was a regular visitor to Hull Fair each October, still with a complete and legible destination blind, seen at various times with different routes displayed. Here it was the 39 to Garden Village. *(R F Mack)*

Part Four - Wartime Motorbuses

As mentioned already, there were two distinct types of wartime bus. The first was that completed from partially built vehicles or from stocks of parts in hand when all bus building was frozen on the outbreak of war; the second was designed to a specification laid down by the Ministry of Supply. Operators had to apply for new buses and allocations were made by the Ministry of War Transport. Hull lost many buses to enemy bombing and needed all the new ones it could get. Thus, between 1941 and 1944, the department took into stock 14 "unfrozen" buses (Nos 190-203 - ten AEC Regents and four Leyland Titans) and 36 "utility" Guy Arabs to MoS specification (Nos 204-39). The bodywork on these vehicles was a mixture of manufacturers and styles and very seldom accorded with what the operator would have preferred. Brush, Northern Counties and Leyland supplied the bodies on Hull's 14 unfrozen buses, for example, and Duple, Massey and Park Royal those on the utility Guys.

Above: Unfrozen AEC Regent No. **194** (**GKH 375**) is seen as delivered with its Brush utility body, devoid of livery and with a full complement of wartime masked lamps and white markings.

Right: Number **196** (**GKH 377**), another AEC Regent, had an all-metal Brush 60-seat body to peacetime standards originally intended for a Coventry Corporation vehicle. From this angle, from behind the coach station crush barriers, Duggleby's toy shop can be seen on the corner across the road. That was another Aladdin's Cave. Happy days... *(Both: Ron Maybray Collection)*

Above: The Northern Counties Motor & Engineering Company supplied bodies to their curvaceous prewar design for three of the unfrozen AEC Regents, Nos 197-9. Only No. **197** (**GKH 378**) kept its original body until withdrawal (in 1963). Although substantially rebuilt in 1948 by the Yorkshire Equipment Company, it retained its original NCME outline. It is seen circa 1961 in the coach station.
Below: Four Leyland Titan TD7 models, Nos 200-3, appeared as the last of the 1942 unfrozen buses. Fitted with Leyland's own bodywork, they were 56-seaters originally intended for the Western SMT, Kilmarnock, fleet. In Hull service they retained the economical Scottish destination screen layout, as shown on No. **200** (**GKH 381**), again in the coach station around 1961. *(Both: Geoffrey Holt)*

Above: This is a poor picture technically, taken from a badly deteriorating negative, but it is so unusual that it simply had to be included. Dating from immediately after the war, it shows the first of the utility Guy Arabs, Duple-bodied No. **204** (**GKH 517**), in streamlined livery; and one of those bodied by Park Royal, No. **222** (**GRH 137**), still in its drab all-over wartime paint.

Below: The other bodybuilder for the utility Guys was Massey Brothers, of Wigan, one of whose bodies is shown on the last of the utility Guys, 1945's No. **239** (**GRH 384**), photographed in the yard at Lombard Street waiting to take up a timing on the 22 to Ellerburn Avenue. *(Both: L R Storry)*

Hull buses destroyed by enemy action[1]

Make and model	Fleet numbers	Totals
Single-deckers		
AEC Regal	1, 6, 8[2], 10	4
Double-deckers		
Leyland Titan TD1	67, 68, 114	3
Leyland Titan TD2	94, 97, 98, 113, 116, 119, 120, 122	8
AEC Regent (petrol)	75, 76, 77, 81, 82, 84, 85	7
AEC Regent (diesel)	128, 181, 185, 186, 188	5
Daimler CP6	103, 105, 106, 107, 108, 109, 111, 138, 142, 144, 145, 146	12
Daimler COG5	14, 154, 157, 158, 160, 165[2], 166, 167	8
	Total[3]	47

Notes:-

[1] – All on 7th/8th May 1941 except No. **103** on 17th July 1941

[2] – The chassis of AEC Regal No. **8** and Daimler COG5 No. **165** were recovered and repaired by AEC at Bradford and rebodied by Roe as single- and double-deck respectively. The latter was unique in being the <u>only</u> Roe double-deck body that was not lowbridge or Beverley Bar-profile highbridge, i.e. it was the only normal Roe highbridge utility.

[3] – On 17th July 1941 a number of other buses were damaged, some, including Daimler CP6 No. **140**, so badly that major repairs were necessary. Number 140 was thus rebuilt by Halifax Corporation.

Forty-seven buses destroyed, and many more severely damaged *(see table above)*, but these six Leyland Titans were among the survivors. Numbers **100**, **123**, **117**, **93/6** and **118** (**RH 6108**, **TF 7827/62**, **RH 6101/4** and **TF 7816**) were at the back of Holderness Road depot in 1949, tired and weary, with just the last journey to the scrapyard before them. *(John Banks Collection)*

Part Five - Wartime Buses Rejuvenated

In common with many other operators, Hull had trouble with some of the utility bodywork, mainly because wartime shortages of seasoned timber had meant the use of "green" wood in its construction. The chassis, on the other hand, remained sound for much longer. From 1948 to 1952 the department rebodied 23 wartime buses; a further five had their original bodies completely rebuilt and eight were repanelled. The rebodyings involved the use of bodies older than their new chassis, a reversal of the usual procedure. The unique photograph above shows three of the 1939 Gardner-engined AEC Regents. The two on the right, Nos **182/3** (**FRH 582/3**), have their original Massey bodies, which were about to be removed and mounted on Guy Arabs Nos 230 and 222. On the left of the group of three is the first of the 1939 batch, No. **170** (**FRH 570**). It has already given up its body to 1942 unfrozen AEC Regent No. 191, whose Brush utility body it has received in exchange. It never ran in this form. To add to the historic interest of this photograph, the single-decker on the left is No. **8** (**RH 4578**), the AEC Regal rebodied with a utility Roe body. *(A D Packer Collection/L R Storry)*

Below: Ten of the rebodyings used the handsome Weymann bodies from the 1937 batch of Daimler COG5s, Nos 11-25. Unfrozen 1942 AEC Regent No. **198** (**GKH 379**) received the body from Daimler No. 17. It is seen here in Jameson Street on the 64/68 routes departure stand, apparently acting as a trolleybus on a short working 68 to East Park. *(L R Storry)*

Upper: The Massey body from 1939 AEC Regent No. 173 was used to rebody 1942 unfrozen Regent No. **196** (**GKH 377**), seen here in Paragon Street in the first weeks of motorbus operation of the former 70 Hessle Road trolleybus route, which was abandoned on 29th January 1961. Behind is a trolleybus on the 69 Anlaby Road route, which would survive until 4th February 1962. (*Geoffrey Holt*)

Centre: Unfrozen AEC Regent No. **193** (**GKH 374**) at Lombard Street garage in 1961. It carries the Massey body formerly carried by No. 172. By a rare coincidence, it is a rear-nearside view, the same angle as seen of the same body on its original chassis on page 64. A comparison will show that the rear destination screen - even then out of use - was eliminated when the body was mounted on No. 193. (*John Banks*)

Lower: An example of the reused Massey bodies from the 1939 AEC Regents on a wartime Guy Arab. Number **222** (**GRH 137**), in the first of a quartet of photographs taken in the coach station on the same day, is seen arriving on the 41 Preston Road route; it has the body from No. 183, seen on its original chassis in the upper picture on page 69. (*Geoffrey Holt*)

Upper: Of the ten ex-Daimler Weymann bodies dating from 1937 that were reused, two went on to unfrozen AEC Regents and eight on to Guy Arab chassis. One of the latter was No. **212** (**GRH 32**), which in this picture was working route 11 to Spring Bank West (Wymersley Road). *(Geoffrey Holt)*

Centre: Guy Arab No. **213** (**GRH 33**) was not rebodied; its Massey utility body was rebuilt in the department's workshops to what was described as "postwar standard" - effectively a new body. The bus was parked in the coach station waiting for a crew to take it over for a route 42 run to Marfleet via New Bridge Road. *(Geoffrey Holt)*

Lower: Yet another variation on the wartime Guy Arab theme is provided by No. **229** (**GRH 170**), which retained its original Park Royal utility body, though it was completely repanelled by the Corporation. After all the rebodyings, rebuildings and repanellings, there remained eleven Guy Arabs that received no special treatment and which were, generally, withdrawn earlier. To round off this complicated story of the 50 wartime Hull buses, Leyland TD7 No. 202 was repanelled in 1952: the other three remained original; and of the ten wartime AECs, nine were rebodied and one was rebuilt. *(Geoffrey Holt)*

Part Six - Early Postwar Motorbuses

Above: The first postwar buses were 16 AEC Regent II models in 1946. As the supply situation eased the various government ministries relinquished their stranglehold and Hull was again able to specify bodywork from Weymann. The buses were 60-seaters and had manual gearboxes. Number **247** (**HAT 247**) is seen in the coach station. *(Geoffrey Holt)*

Below: The following year 24 more AEC Regents arrived, again with Weymann bodies, this time seating 58. These buses were the Regent III model and had preselector gearboxes and fluid flywheels. The two batches were easily told apart, especially if one could hear the transmission, and there were detail differences in the body, particularly round the cab front. Number **277** (**HRH 477**) is illustrated. *(Geoffrey Holt)*

Above: In 1949 and 1950 further AEC Regent IIIs were bought: Weymann 58-seaters again, but to the then newly permitted width of eight feet - the 1946/7 batches were 7ft 6ins. There were 56 of the new roomier buses, with KAT and KRH registrations, and they were the "face" of the Corporation's bus fleet for many years. Number **296** (**KAT 296**) was photographed in 1961 in Spring Bank West on a route 12 timing to Wold Road. *(John Banks)*

Below: A small batch of single-deckers on the AEC Regal chassis with Weymann 35-seat front-entrance bodywork joined the fleet in 1949. Numbers 1-6 were registered KKH 646-51 and renumbered 151-6 in 1956. The first three are seen in line at Lombard Street in 1961, having been converted in 1954 for driver-only operation. *(John Banks)*

Above: The last AEC Regents to be bought new - there were to be many second-hand ones - were six Mark III models with Weymann 58-seat bodywork in 1953. The body design was known as the "Aurora" and the then controversial concealed radiator styling contributed to a very striking appearance. The last of them, No. **341** (**OKH 341**), was in Lombard Street in 1961, heading for Ferensway and eventually Ings Road on route 40. *(John Banks)*

Below: A 7ft 6ins-wide Regent, No. **265** (**HRH 465**); an 8ft-wide successor, No. **291** (**KAT 291**); and a "tin-front" Aurora, No. **336** (**OKH 336**), are contrasted in this fortuitous line-up at Lombard Street in about 1960 - the 98 route was a special football service introduced in 1959 and withdrawn the following year. *(R F Mack)*

Part Seven - Second-hand Motorbuses

Left: A method of saving costs - by not having to pay conductors' wages - and of easing recruitment problems, was to make the driver collect the fares. Hull was very early in the field with a firm decision to convert to 100% driver-only operation, using the Leyland Atlantean, which had a rear engine and front doorway and was introduced in 1959. While it was building up a fleet of such vehicles, Hull had no wish to commit itself to buying new traditional buses and so made use of large numbers of front-engined, rear-entrance AECs and Daimlers, purchased second-hand from other municipalities. The first to come, in 1961, were ten Daimler CVG6s from Newcastle Corporation, one of which, Metro-Cammell-bodied No. **125** (**KVK 966**), is seen in Portland Street outside the department's offices, soon after its repaint into Hull colours. *(John Banks)*

Below: The Daimlers were followed, in 1962, by 19 AEC Regent RTs from St Helens Corporation. With Park Royal bodies seating 56, these vehicles were identical in every respect except livery to the London Transport RT class, which totalled 4,825. For service in Hull, the destination screens, which St Helens had ordered to the London Transport specification, were rebuilt as shown on No. **131** (**BDJ 811**). The photograph was taken at the former trolleybus terminus at Chanterlands Avenue North in 1962. It was on route 23, which had replaced trolleybus route 61 on 29th July 1962. *(John Banks)*

These pictures, taken at Holderness Road depot on 24th March 1968, neatly encapsulate what was going on in Hull in the 1960s as the front-engined fleet was kept afloat through massive second-hand purchases of other operators' redundant vehicles, at the same time as new Leyland Atlanteans for driver-only operation were arriving as fast as they could be afforded. In the upper picture is No. **102** (**FBC 283**), a 1949 Metro-Cammell-bodied AEC Regent, one of twelve bought from Leicester City Transport in 1966 when they were 17 years old. On the right in the lower picture is an ex-Nottingham City Transport AEC Regent yet to be repainted and still identifiable as Nottingham No. **190** (**OTV 190**) in green and cream livery; it stands alongside ex-Nottingham **OTV 138**, now repainted blue and white and numbered **158** in the Hull fleet. A total of 36 of these Park Royal-bodied AECs came from Nottingham. At the far left is a Leyland Atlantean No. **386** (**7386 RH**), showing well the front entrance, which could easily - it was thought - be controlled by the driver. *(Both: John Banks)*

Part Eight - Underfloor and Rear Engines

Above: In 1957-60 fifteen AEC Reliance underfloor-engined buses with Weymann dual-doorway bodies were acquired. One of the 1957 vehicles, No. **163** (**WAT 163**) is seen laying over on the waste ground in Canning Street after a journey on the Sutton Hospital route 35. Note the "Pay as you enter" sign. Conductors are beginning to disappear. *(John Banks)*

Below: How would the streamlined livery look on a modern rear-engined bus? Very well, if brand new No. **343** (**6343 KH**) is any guide. This was the second Leyland Atlantean, one of five delivered in May 1960: the first 30ft-long, 8ft-wide vehicles in the fleet; they had a seating capacity of 75. *(Hull Daily Mail)*

Part Nine - Buses and Bridges

Hull's bridges are - like the trams - worthy of a book fully as long as this one all to themselves. The main ones traversed by the bus and trolleybus services - and the trams before them - are the tidal bridges spanning the River Hull and the railway bridges over the various thoroughfares. These days, so far as river crossings are concerned, matters have been eased by the opening of Garrison Way and Myton Bridge close to the mouth of the Hull.

This page upper: There was a ferry across the Hull in mediaeval times, to the north of the present North Bridge, and in 1541 a bridge was built, just to the south of it. That old bridge, in more recent times, carried tram tracks and so must certainly have been rebuilt or even replaced *in situ*, perhaps more than once. It was approached via Charlotte Street, now truncated just short of the river, and was replaced by the present magnificent structure in 1931.

The new bridge was wider and joined George Street to Witham in a straighter line, in effect making Jameson Street, George Street, Witham and Holderness Road virtually a straight road from Paragon Square right out to the city boundary; the western end of that route is now Freetown Way. Even in the fifties and sixties there was considerable congestion on most of the route until the dual carriageway that formerly housed reserved tram tracks was reached. The picture was taken on opening day, 10th August 1931; trams **63** on the Holderness Road "H" route and **87** on the "M" to Hedon Road (Marfleet) star, as does an East Yorkshire Leyland Lion, No. **79** (**WF 1152**), on its way to Sutton via Ings Road. *(Hull Daily Mail)*

Opposite page centre: About 25 years later, Sunbeam W trolleybus No. **79** (**GRH 355**) crosses North Bridge. The trolleybus overhead wires were carried in trunking in the centre of the bridge and when trolleybuses kept to the nearside the trolley poles were almost at right angles to the vehicle's longitudinal axis. *(Hull Daily Mail)*

<< Opposite page lower: Underneath the bridge was a place of extreme light and shade that was very photogenic on sunny days. This April 1956 picture on just such an occasion shows the

overhead wiring to better advantage. Leyland TB7 No. **60** (**FRH 560**) was being kept by its driver a little way out from the extreme nearside and thus the trolley poles were not at such an exaggerated angle as could be the case. *(John Banks Collection/G H F Atkins)*

This page upper: The preceding three pictures were taken from the east side of North Bridge. This view is from the town side, and shows one of the 1963 Leyland Atlanteans, No. **371** (**3371 RH**), running into town from Bilton Grange on the 48 route. *(R F Mack)*

Page 79 centre and lower: Drypool Bridge - closer to the mouth of the Hull - was the other major town centre crossing before Myton Bridge. A narrow structure, there was no room on it for a cyclist to be overtaken, as demonstrated by unfrozen AEC Regent No. **199** (**GKH 380**) with its prewar Weymann body. The lower view includes postwar Regent No. **270** (**HRH 470**) as well as a characterful Austin A40 ice-cream van of Star Dairies registered **KKH 940**. *(R F Mack)*

This page upper: In 1961 the new, much wider, Drypool Bridge was opened. Five buses - three of the new Leyland Atlanteans, a 1946 AEC Regent and a rebodied wartime Guy Arab - are seen on clearance and weight tests on 3rd July 1961. *(G M O'Connell)*

This page centre: The tiny Scott Street bridge over the River Hull was a tight fit for a double-decker on the 40 via Dansom Lane and attempts were made to schedule

7ft 6ins-wide buses where possible. On this occasion, however, 8ft-wide AEC Regent No. **335** (**KRH 345**) was on the route. *(R F Mack)*

<< Opposite page lower: The lifting bridge across the Hull in Sutton Road was close to one of the writer's boyhood homes and naturally was out of bounds to us kids because of the danger of us falling into the river: just as naturally we played there most days. Number **160** (**WAT 160**), a 1957 AEC Reliance, was on the only route, in those days, that crossed this bridge: the 19. *(A D Packer Collection/L R Storry)*

This page: The Hull and Barnsley Railway system of lines built on embankments, which had the excellent effect of obviating the need for level crossings, crossed - among other roads - Beverley Road (near Ryde Avenue), Newland Avenue (near De Grey Street) and Chanterlands Avenue at Murrayfield Road. In the upper view in a splendid period piece from before the First World War, tram No. **92** on the "B" route makes its sedate way into town. The centre picture is of Crossley No. **29** (**ERH 29**) heading in on the 62; much of Newland Avenue can be seen through the bridge. The Chanterlands Avenue bridge was a more substantial affair with central supports dividing the carriageway. The road dipped down below this bridge and was prone to flooding. Crossley **28** (**ERH 28**) is heading for the 61 terminus on 28th July 1957. *(John Banks Collection; L R Storry; A D Packer Collection/L R Storry)*

Part Ten - A Miscellany

Above: This vehicle was not unique in having ended its life as a mobile theatre and bandstand, but it was certainly very unusual. AEC Regal **RH 4758**, formerly No. 8 in the bus fleet, was the one that was rebodied by Roe during the war. On withdrawal circa 1949 it was converted as seen here for use by the Leisure Services Department (known at that time as the Parks and Cemeteries Department). The writer recalls being among an audience of enthralled children watching a performance from the stage of this vehicle on a bombed site in a side street off Newland Avenue in about 1951.

Below: Nineteen-fifty AEC Regent No. **326** (**KRH 336**) in the not-often illustrated situation of being partly raised on a hydraulic lift. *(Both: L R Storry)*

The sign on the bus terminus reads:

KINGSTON UPON HULL
CORPORATION TRANSPORT
MOTORBUS TERMINUS
47 MARFLEET
VIA HEDON RD & EASTERN DOCKS
巴士站往石馬豆面
AUTOBUSES AU PORT DE L'ESTE
OMNIBUSSE ZUM OSTHAVEN
АВТОБУСЫ К ВОСТОЧНЫМ ДОКАМ
AUTOBUSES DIRECCION AL MUELLES DEL ESTE
BUSSAR TILL DE ÖSTRA DOCKORNA
یہ بس ڈاک کی طرف جاتی ہے

POLICE NOTICE
NO PARKING

Multi-language bus stops are also not often seen: they were even rarer in the 1950s and this eight-language example in Savile Street was an endless source of fascination. The 47 to Marfleet served the city's major docks and so had a high percentage of non-English-speaking passengers from among the Merchant Marine whose ships happened to be berthed. The city centre pubs were liable to resound to exotic accents of all sorts, which never seemed to have any trouble in ordering a pint of Hull Brewery bitter or a double Scotch. The bus on this occasion was one of the 1953 Weymann Aurora-bodied AEC Regents, No. **340 (OKH 340)**. A splendid picture, full of nostalgia: the bus was standing more or less outside Gough & Davy's music shop, which is still there. In the 1950s its record department was downstairs and many a brittle, shellac 78 was bought there, their 6/7½d (33p) cost saved with difficulty from 3/6d (17½p) a week pocket money; across the road on the corner with George Street was a coffee merchant, whose products filled the air with the most memorable aroma; just around the corner was Brown's bookshop, also still there, in which many a happy hour was spent browsing among books whose price was even harder to scrape up. And so on...   *(Hull Daily Mail)*

Demonstrators

Bus manufacturers always had one or more chassis bodied and made available for demonstration to potential buyers. Salesmen would use the offer of the loan of such a bus as part of their inducements and some strange liveries were seen in towns and cities. Sometimes an order would result but more often the salesman would retire disappointed. In July 1958 I recall waiting for the 15 to town and being surprised when a red and cream double-decker turned up. It was an AEC all right, but quite unlike anything in Hull's fleet. The vehicle was **76 MME** *(above)*, an AEC Bridgemaster fitted with a Crossley 72-seat body. In this picture it was at Greenwood Avenue, perhaps about to start the very trip on which I rode on it. Although East Yorkshire bought some Bridgemasters, the Corporation did not. A year or so later, in September 1959, Leyland Atlantean demonstrator **398 JTB** was tried. In this view *(below)* it was in Cottingham Road about to turn right into Cottingham Grove - which would have been a tight fit for a 30ft-long by 8ft-wide bus, dimensions not hitherto much experienced by Corporation drivers. Leyland's salesman had more success; the Bridgemaster was an impressive vehicle, of integral construction (i.e. no separate chassis), but it really stood no chance at all - it needed a conductor - and Hull went in for the Atlantean - which had the potential of not incurring that expense - in a big way. *(Both: R F Mack)*

Interiors

There was something about the interior of a traditional bus or trolleybus: the look, the touch, even - when it was new - the smell, that today's plastic and metal concoctions can never match. Earlier, the trams, of course, were different again, with their lavish areas of varnished wood. The layout of a traditional, rear-entrance, front-engined double-decker was very different, too. One boarded from the open back platform and found a seat inside or on top, or, if the bus were full, one might stand inside. With all 58 seats taken and eight standees, the conductor would sternly declare "full up", sometimes adding the time-honoured "there's another one just behind" (whether there was or not), ring the bell three times, and off the bus would go, not stopping until somebody wanted to alight.

Upper: The lower deck looking forward in a 1932 Leyland Titan TD2, No. **104** (**TF 7816**). The padded, upholstered seating was supremely comfortable and spacious: the bus had only 48 seats. (*John Banks Collection*)

Centre: One of the 1937 Leyland 54-seat Weymann-bodied trolleybuses. The upper deck, looking rearwards in this view, was rather sombre but was in quiet good taste. It was a long walk from the front seat and down the stairs: stops in Hull were often closely spaced, and one often had to be nippy to avoid being carried on to the next stop. (*John Banks Collection*)

Lower: Upstairs looking forward on an ex-Nottingham Park Royal-bodied AEC Regent, No. **183** (**OTV 191**). (*Philip Battersby*)

Part Eleven - Into the Modern Era

Above: The new Leyland Atlanteans stood out as something quite alien among the traditional Weymann-bodied AEC Regents, as shown in this view of No. **361** (**9361 AT**) in the coach station. *Below:* Atlantean No. **382** (**7382 RH**) alongside ex-St Helens AEC Regent RT No. **139** (**BDJ 825**) in the coach station on 7th July 1969. Both were on recently introduced circular services - another sign of the times. *(Geoffrey Holt; Philip Battersby)*

Above: The streamlined livery sat reasonably comfortably on the slab-fronted, box-like Leyland Atlanteans as long as the front panels were largely occupied by destination screens, as seen on No. **375** (**3375 RH**) in Paragon Street on 12th October 1972. The vehicle alongside was No. **255** (**PRH 255G**) from a batch delivered in 1969. The screens were lower, narrower and wider, leaving the white swoop of the livery unbroken and rather prominent. *(Philip Battersby)*

Below: Also in 1969, the first of the twin-door Atlanteans arrived, epitomised by No. **268** (**TKH 268H**). This style of bus for many years formed the backbone of Cottingham Road depot's allocation for the 15C/17C Orchard Park circulars. *(Hull Daily Mail)*

A notable event in 1964 was the arrival in the fleet of the first 36ft-long single-decker. Number **172** (**BKH 172B**) was a Leyland Panther, with rear engine and twin-door bodywork by Charles Roe, who were also bodying Hull's contemporary Atlanteans. Six more Panthers would follow in 1965 and a further five in 1966. They lasted reasonably well, being withdrawn between 1980 and 1982, despite the Panther generally not being among the most successful Leyland models: nor, for that matter, was the Atlantean in its early form, but Hull's engineers seemed to make them work better than - for example - London Transport, which had a disastrous experience with a batch of 50 in 1965/6. Number 172 was in Annandale Road in the rain on a murky 24th March 1968; it was operating the almost circular 10 route from Gipsyville to Marfleet. This particular bus was exhibited at the 1964 Commercial Motor Show. It was lent to Southport Corporation from April to June 1965. Upon withdrawal in 1982 it went for preservation to the Hull Transport Museum. *(Both: John Banks)*

Numbers **72** (**BKH 172B**) and **79** (**GAT 179D**), from 1964 and 1966, were, by the late seventies when these pictures were taken, among the last Leyland Panthers in public service in the country, and by then they were not often seen out. A journey they did sometimes work up to the end of their existence was a single rush-hour timing on works service 45. The location is the British Petroleum Company's Saltend refinery, the outer terminus of the route. (*Both: John Banks*)

Above: Eight new Leyland Atlanteans in 1964 were the first Hull double-deckers to have the new suffix registrations. The suffix scheme started in 1963 with the letter "A", but few issuing authorities used it; most began in 1964 with "B" and a few, Leeds for example, waited until 1965 and "C". Number **402** (**BAT 402B**) was brand new in this picture at Cottingham Road depot. It had the usual 75-seat bodywork by Roe. At that stage still crew-operated, its driver and conductor were smartly kitted out in proper uniforms and collars and ties. *(L R Storry)*

Below: There was a fairly long transitional period during which the streamlined livery could be seen alongside the more modern version that replaced it, but there are few colour photographs of both together. Atlanteans Nos **170** (**3370 RH**), **169** (**3369 RH**) and **161** (**9361 AT**) were displaying blinds for various route 10 workings. *(John Banks)*

Upper: Hull's last order for new Leyland Atlanteans was for 15 of the revised AN68 model for 1982 delivery. These came as a surprise after Hull had bought no fewer than 60 Scania- or Gardner-powered double-deckers from Metro-Cammell between 1975 and 1981. Among the last Atlanteans to be built, they had, as might have been expected for Hull, bodywork by Roe. Number **372** (**WAG 372X**) is illustrated, thought to be in East Park. *(KHCT)*

Centre: A batch of five minibuses based on Ford A type chassis appeared in 1976. Not really buses at all, but rather converted delivery vans, they were found wanting and all had gone by 1981. Number **12** (**MAT 12P**) was the second of the batch, photographed at Stepney station. *(KHCT)*

Lower: Here is one of the Scania/Metro-Cammell buses referred to above. Number **428** (**WKH 428S**) was at the bleak Bransholme terminus of the 39 route in the winter of 1979. *(John Banks)*

Apart from sophisticated new vehicles, driver-only operation and revised route networks to serve an expanding city, progress "Into the Modern Era" also brought the twin problems of staff/management relations and vandalism. In the picture above, buses had come temporarily off service in 1979 and were parked in Spring Street so that drivers could attend a mass meeting. Leyland Atlantean No. **224** (**JRH 424E**) of 1967 was the last vehicle in the line of ten. The random arrival of the buses had nonetheless resulted in a neat division between the first seven with side advertisements and the last three without: the latter's appearance was smarter and much improved for the lack. Vandalism took its worst turn in the seventies in a series of arson attacks. Two Atlanteans were lost to an arsonist on 9th September 1973 and later in the decade two similar attacks exactly a year apart, on 11th March of 1978 and 1979, further decimated the ranks of the older Atlanteans. All three incidents involved buses parked on the open ground, colloquially known as "the Muck", in Short Street, behind the coach station. The picture below graphically illustrates the extent of the damage on the 1979 occasion. Numbers **166**, **186/9/0** (**9366 AT**, **7386/9/0 RH**) are shown. Number 189 is believed to have been repaired and to have run again. The other three had to be scrapped. *(Both: John Banks)*

Above: Fire brigade equipment and personnel in preventative action on 12th March 1979. The remains of the burnt-out buses were being closely examined to ensure that nothing was still smouldering and likely to cause a fresh outbreak of fire. Numbers **166** and **186** again. *(John Banks)*
Below: Somewhat poignantly, an advertisement reading "Come home to a <u>real</u> fire" was being carried by No. **189 (7389 RH)** at this time. In this photograph taken on 12th March 1979, it can be seen that the damage, though visibly very bad, was restricted to the front bay; No. 180 alongside was in a much worse state. *(John Banks)*

Above: After Hull had taken 30 Metro-Camell-bodied Scania Metropolitans into stock, that model was discontinued and the bodybuilder introduced a new model, the Metrobus, again using Scania running units, and Gardner engines: Hull bought 30 in two batches of 15 each in 1980 and 1981. The last of the first batch, No. **515** (**LAT 515V**), was in Beverley High Road, opposite the former Endsleigh College, on 18th April 1991. Behind was No. **367** (**GAT 206N**), a 1975 Atlantean. The pictures on this page illustrate a revised version of the blue and white livery. *(John Banks)*

Below: Following the batches of Metrobuses, and with the Atlantean no longer available, Hull turned to the Dennis Dominator, a chassis make that had last been purchased in the early 1930s. Number **104** (**B104 UAT**) was one of a 1984 batch of ten. It was in Beverley High Road, in almost the same place, on 23rd August 1990. *(John Banks)*

Above: The difficulties facing Hull's passenger transport undertaking following deregulation have been outlined in the Introduction. The measures resorted to in attempts to stave off the inevitable included marketing the buses as the "Blue & Whites" and exhorting citizens to use them. MCW No. **530** (**SAG 530W**) displays the branding on its front panels. Alongside, similar vehicle No. **514** (**LAT 514V**) has a revised livery of blue, white and yellow, following sale to Cleveland Transit, and the "KHCT" logo is in the latter's style - all somewhat weakening the "Blue & Whites" message on the remaining pre-Cleveland-liveried buses. *(John Banks)*

Below: East Lancashire-bodied Dennis Dominator No. **132** (**E132 SAT**), new in 1987, was damaged by fire in 1991 and was rebodied by the same coachbuilder as a 76-seat dual-door vehicle for use on the King George Dock shuttle in connection with North Sea Ferries sailings, a duty previously carried out by one of the two-door Atlanteans. Alongside was No. **133** (**E133 SAT**) with the style of single-door body previously carried by No. 132. *(John Banks)*

Above: Further attempts to regain financial stability involved the purchase of a fleet of coaches for private hire, excursion and tours work under the name "Kingstonian". Typical of the vehicles used for this operation was **BUT 25Y**, a 1983 Dennis with Plaxton 49-seat coachwork. All-over advertising on buses in the mid 1990s was no new thing, but had not been seen much in Hull. Dennis Dominator No. **131** (**C131 CAT**) was thus decked out for the Brooke Tile Superstore. The "Blue & Whites" motto sat uneasily with such a bold colour scheme that had no blue in it. Alongside was a real Blue & White, MCW No. **530** (**SAG 530W**). The photograph was taken on the parking area at the back of the coach station on 10th May 1995. *(John Banks)*

Below: In 1984 a Gardner-engined Leyland National adapted for the carriage of wheelchairs was acquired. It operated a weekly schedule of special routes for the disabled with the fleetname "Handyrider" and had the same livery as the Kingstonian coaches. Number **60** (**B60 WKH**) is seen in Carr Lane outside the Cecil cinema on 11th May 1995. *(John Banks)*

Above: The Swedish Scania *marque* was turned to again in the last years of the undertaking, including in 1988 a batch of six 49-seat dual-purpose vehicles with East Lancashire Coachbuilders bodywork. The dual-purpose concept in theory fitted them for use either on bus routes or as coaches but all were later converted as 50-seat service buses. Number **706** (**F706 CAG**) was the last of the six. It was photographed at Carr Lane, turning into Ferensway, on 11th May 1995. *(John Banks)*

Below: On that occasion the very next vehicle to pass the camera was one of the last batch of buses to be purchased by Hull before the transport undertaking was sold to Cleveland Transit. From a batch of eight Scania double-deckers with 84-seat bodies from East Lancashire is illustrated No. **811** (**H811 WKH**). Eighty-four seats! - a far cry from the 34-seat Saurer double-deckers of 1909, or even from the 58-seat AEC Regents of the writer's youth. And so ends the story of the trams, trolleybuses and motorbuses of one of the proudest of the British municipal fleets. Nowadays the three crowns have disappeared from the sides of Hull's buses, which look just like those of Manchester or Middlesbrough or dozens of other towns and cities. *(John Banks)*

Part Twelve - Pure Nostalgia...

It is not certain whether the memory or photography is the *fons et origo* of nostalgia: the memory can play tricks and the camera can lie (certainly in this age of digital manipulation), but they are all we have and perhaps nostalgia is a combination of both. Two developments in the second half of the last century were a great help to transport enthusiasts wanting to record and appreciate what had gone before: the availability of affordable colour photography of an acceptable quality; and the willingness of bus operators to resurrect their former liveries on the occasion of anniversaries. In the last seven pages of this book, let us simply give ourselves up to nostalgia.

Hull's buses and the trams before them had been municipally operated since the inauguration of the electric trams in 1899; in 1989 it was decided to commemorate the 90th anniversary visually on the streets of the city by repainting three buses, one in each of the earlier liveries: the original maroon and cream, the ex-Dundee "Morrison" blue and white of 1932 and Mr Lawson's 1936 streamlined; three of the newest double-deckers, the 1987 Dennis Dominators, were used. Numbers **137/6/5 (E137/6/5 SAT)** - in that order - display those historic liveries in views taken behind the coach station (137) and in Alfred Gelder Street (136) on 27th April 1990, and in Prospect Street (135) on 12th July 1989. The picture of No. 137 includes one of the "Royale" minibuses. *(All: John Banks)*

<< *Opposite page:* Hull's trams finally vanished from the streets in 1945, and no colour images of them in service have been traced. However, preserved and beautifully restored car No. **132** gives an excellent impression of how splendid they looked. *(John Banks)*

This page: Some British trolleybus systems disappeared before the advent of cheap, reliable colour photography, Hull's thankfully not among them. These views from the winter of 1962/3 are of Sunbeam W No. **88** (**HRH 88**) in Jameson Street *(above)* and Coronation No. **109** (**RKH 109**) *(below)* in King Edward Street. *(John Banks)*

To have colour photographs - however amateurish - of the wartime chassis and the early postwar Weymann-bodied AEC Regents is most gratifying. The 1942 unfrozen Regent double-decker in postwar rebodied (ex-a 1939 Regent) form is represented *(above)* by No. **195 (GKH 376)** at Central depot, Lombard Street in the snows of the 1962/3 winter. Ahead of it - and also seen below - is No. **217 (GRH 132)**, one of the 1944 utility Guy Arabs later rebodied with 1937 ex-Daimler Weymann bodies in 1948. Both vehicles were withdrawn in 1963. It is worth stressing that the bodies on these buses take us back to the prewar period. *(Both: John Banks)*

Above: The very early postwar AEC Regents, delivered in 1946 as Nos 240-55, were, as previously mentioned, fitted with manual gearboxes, which gave them an unmistakeable musical transmission sound: this was so characteristic, in fact, that it was easy to identify one before it came round the corner. Number **253 (HAT 253)** and all but one of the rest of the batch survived into 1966. Here it is at Holderness Road depot in 1962, with, in the background, poles and wires of the turning circle for the soon-to-disappear trolleybuses. *(John Banks)*

Below: A later view of the parking area behind Holderness Road depot on 24th March 1968 managed to catch three categories of AEC Regent: Hull's own Weymann-bodied examples (the later, preselector-gearbox type), an ex-Leicester machine (with its back to the camera) and two ex-Nottingham buses (at extreme left and right) with that on the left still in Nottingham livery. A Leyland Atlantean represents the next generation. *(John Banks)*

Above: The London Transport-designed RT took well to Hull's streamlined livery. Ex-St Helens No. **133** (**BDJ 816**) is seen at Central depot, Lombard Street. *(John Banks)*

Below: For the last picture in the book (apart from the covers), it was difficult to resist this look inside Cottingham Road depot. This is 1962 and the tramlines, last used before the war, were still evident. The view replicates that which we kids used to have in the early fifties as we peeped in, looking down the endless lines of blue and white swoops and whirls, hoping to see a newly delivered Coronation trolleybus or - even better - be allowed in by a sympathetic foreman to look for bus tickets and just wander around, drinking it all in. Couldn't happen today... *(John Banks)*